The Sophisticated Guide to
Simplifying and Managing
Your Workload and More

DANIELLE E. FELTON

teach and
go home

teach and go home

The Sophisticated Guide to Simplifying and
Managing Your Workload and More

Difference Press, Washington, D.C., USA
© Danielle Felton, 2021

ISBN: 978-1-68309-286-5

No part of this publication in any form should be considered medical advice.

Cover Design: Jennifer Stimson
Interior Book Design: Kozakura
Editing: Emily Tuttle
Author's photo courtesy of Darryl Scot

Stepping Stone
It turns out you were right. This one is because of you.
Mom, I will love you always.

Table of Contents

CHAPTER 1
"Help Please, I'm a Teacher" – The Realization   1

CHAPTER 2
"I Teach, We Teach, Are We All Failing Together?"   13

CHAPTER 3
"Objectives, Please" – A Framework and Overview   31

CHAPTER 4
"Class Begins" –PPOP Classroom: How to
Structure a Simplified Functionality and Design   39

CHAPTER 5
"PIG, PPOP, Instruct!" – How to Effectively
PPOP in Instructional Planning   83

CHAPTER 6
"The Professional Triplets and Dynamics of
Professionalism and Communication"   107

CHAPTER 7

"Clock in, Clock out" – Home, Work, Life, and Balance   139

CHAPTER 8

"Give Me Recess or Give Me Retirement"
– Exiting and Transitions   157

CHAPTER 9

"Over the Hill or over the Mountain
We Conquer Both Together!" – Obstacles You
May Face and How to Overcome Them   173

CHAPTER 10

"Dismissal Bell Rings" – The Conclusion   179

Acknowledgments   183

Thank You for Reading   185

About the Author   187

About Difference Press   191

Other Books by Difference Press   195

CHAPTER 1

"Help Please, I'm a Teacher"
– The Realization

Hello, teacher! How are you? My name is Danielle – I am a teacher too, and I absolutely love everything about teaching. I love the teachers, the hustle, the planning, the learning, the achieving. I love the fight, the change, and the passion. Most of all, I love, love, love my students. I have loved and cared for each and every one who has come through my doors as if they were my own. My very own concern, my very own achievement, my very own responsibility. Teaching has been a dream and a goal of mine since I was a little girl, ever since I met my very first kindergarten teacher. She was amazing and made it look so easy. All of my elementary school teachers did and were phenomenal. I was blessed, encouraged, and inspired. So, I took the duty on myself.

Teaching and what it takes to teach involve so much more than teacher-student interactions. Teaching is also planning and preparing for the actual act of instructing. It is the outcome, and everything else you do prior are the equations and addends.

When I began teaching, it was with huge ambition. I thought that I could literally take it all on and still maintain my life and free time too.

I was right, and it was true – I could do it, but I was completely wrong in how to go about it. I was completely overwhelmed and drowning in paperwork, grades, to-do lists, and emails, not to mention the lesson planning I had to do in order to actually teach and be ready for the next day. It was as if I had two or more completely different jobs and each was a priority. I felt like I could never catch up no matter how hard I tried, how much effort I put in, or how late I stayed up planning. Even still, I would refuse to give up. This was my dream, and if I had to fight to keep it, then I was going to have to fight for it! In the end, I almost completely burnt out and faced indefinite defeat. Sound familiar?

It was by no accident that I became a teacher. It was a position I pursued and was committed to. Becoming a teacher was my dream. My passion is what gave me the confidence to believe that the unbelievable amount of work I was facing each day could and would be handled because that was exactly what I was going to do – handle it. In my youthful and naive mind, I thought, "Come on, how hard could it actually be to put some papers in a labeled folder and write important dates on a calendar? I am a teacher; I can do anything. I certainly can figure out a way to get this work managed and under control."

Through a blurred macro-lens, that assumption was not entirely untrue. Rather, it was unrealistic, more or less. Like you may already know, dear reader, teachers have practical superpowers that most people can only dream of. We are masters and learners in all things. We are the miners, the jewelers, and the many steps in between. We are developers, producers, and creatives. We do all these things out of love and honor and make others think we do it all with ease and little effort.

The respectable traits of our profession are devotion, detail, and efficiency. We are all amazing, and it is amazing to be a teacher. It is a sorely uncelebrated fact that teachers rock. Literally, they are full-on rock stars – rock-out, guitar-smashing, drum-solo rock stars. Just swap the early mornings and late nights partying and in the studio, being on stage with a microphone in front of thousands of fans for early mornings and late nights planning, grading, and preparing for a classroom. Swap the microphone for an expo, add a carpet and whiteboard backdrop, reduce the crowd to an even thirty, and we are not too far off. As far as the press and interviews, consider those observations and parent-teacher conferences.

As for fame and publicity, come on now! The walk from the parking lot to the front door during drop-off or pickup alone can be a total paparazzi and "Can I get your autograph?" moment in itself. The only difference is the paparazzi are parents and students, and instead of asking for an autograph, they're asking for updates. I must admit, the celebrity moments are some of my favorites.

I too geek out when I see a past teacher of my own. You can't help it – it's just something about seeing one of your favorite teachers. And if they remember you? That'll just make our whole day. And the true teacher in us can't help but love seeing and getting an update on our past students. We always want to know how they've grown and how they are doing.

Still, however thrilling the bounty of fame may be, the best rock stars know when to take a break and retreat. Likewise, the greatest superheroes know when to retreat and recover. You must because it is

3

essential for your heart (physically), your passion (spiritually), and your capacity to do (mentally). However super, capable, and talented you may be, you can still take a break or ask for help. We know these things; this is not new knowledge. Then why do we teachers still feel conflicted about prioritizing and taking care of yourself first? Constantly pushing ourselves onto the backburner of our lives. We get so consumed in our work and our practices that we don't realize how much it costs to push ourselves through. We overlook and do not take heed to those subtle backburning flames until we are on the verge of burning out! One day, you look out into the space of your classroom and realize that it has transitioned from 'my passion' to 'my job.' When the work of teaching starts to outweigh the joy and compromising your ability to perform, it is time for major change. I also suspect that is why you picked up this book, and I am so glad you did. Whether you are at the point of change, creeping towards the door, or just checking for a friend, I am glad you are here because here is where you will redefine the weights and balance the distribution of work requirements and responsibilities to balance the scale of your life and return to or create a meaningful life with time and space for you to fill it full of joy, passion, value, and fun while you work along the way.

YOUR SUPERPOWERS: MENTAL CAPACITY

I'm a teacher too. I understand what it is like to have eighty-two different first and last names, along with the various family traits and nuances that belong to each memorized and ready for recall at any given moment. We don't fret at the idea of being expected to provide specific and accurate information about each one of our students at the drop of a dime.

You're responsible for knowing that William only likes to be called William and never Will because if you call him such, William will become stubborn and have a fit. You have to remember that Laila must be reminded and dismissed to go to the nurse before lunch each day at 12:15, and she must take a partner with her, but her partner can never be Kaitlyn, unless Laila chooses Kaitlyn, because Laila and Kaitlyn have a 'protocol' put into place from a disagreement they had last school year that is being carried over into this school year by their new teacher, because they have both been placed in the same class again. This is not unusual.

There's the pressure of an observation in two weeks, the grading window closing in three days, two assessments to give, grade, enter into the grade book, and return with feedback. Plus, it's flu season, and your throat is scratchy. How about the days when you have lesson plans to develop or prep, twelve emails pending (four of which belong to Laila's mom and two more from other staff members involving William), a parent phone call to return, a spontaneous bloody nose, a fire drill, and two staff meetings disguised under the names 'team' and 'committee' meeting on the same day? How about within the same afternoon? How far off is that description?

Wait, I have one more – this is one of my favorites. That beautiful morning when all things are going right and you open your email to find that one beautiful email that we all love to find:

Subject line: Changes to Schedule: Please Read

Good morning, Fantastic Teacher,

I know how much time and effort you have dedicated to your lesson plans this week. The amount of respect and effort you have given to maintain your expected curriculum pace and the district's expectations of you have not gone unnoticed. In fact, I am just so thrilled with how fantastic you are, we (powers higher than you) have decided to disregard your schedule and curriculum timeline for [insert disruption of choice] because why not? It shouldn't be that big of a bother to you at all, Superstar. You've got this! See you in the cafeteria with your class at [insert inconvenient time]. Can't wait, what an opportunity, super fun!

Sincerely,
Administration
Committed to Every Student's Success (by any means necessary).

Please forgive my sarcasm right there. It is pessimistic and unproductive, to say the least. These types of unplanned things are to be taken seriously. But however beneficial and exciting these events may be, does the educator get a calendar date extension? Does the window for test preparation readiness include a ninety-minute assembly? When it does, the event is grandly anticipated and an event we look forward to. When it is not, it is not.

The calendar due dates and days allotted for pacing don't change. It is an unanticipated burden and often received as a complete disregard of and unappreciation for the work ethic and effort we put forth each day. In my most honest reflections, it is also a very real *sometimes* interpretation of the feelings I get when I receive information that makes me feel as if the efforts I have put forth in professionalism and for student achievement are completely skipped over for last-minute 'fun' ideas. This is not to forget that it can also be an instructional time deficit that the educator now has to revise and re-plan the planned plan to make up for the loss.

I don't always get gripey, but when I do, I gripe sarcastically. Forgive me. There are other times, especially in June, when I am hand-raising ready to volunteer my class, classroom, and services for 'fun' ideas. Timing is everything, and planning for the timing is even better. No matter, in a manner of the time it takes to process the information and reorganize it our super teacher minds', we will rearrange our entire day to now include a twenty-five to fifty-minute assembly, guest speaker, announcement, etc., and still manage to deliver our lessons and objectives too.

These are just a few of the subtle unspoken dynamics of the teacher experience. I told you we were super. It's the practical superpowers and dynamics we possess for the fluidity of our classroom, the success of our students, and our instructional flow.

And all of these things are mostly out of our control. Ironically, as controlling as teachers can be, most of the teaching involves things we cannot and would never be able to control. But lack of control is not the enemy or the cure. It is the ability to control what you can so that you can flow among and between what you can't.

I could spend forever making complaints about how Laila and Kaitlyn should not be in the same class anyway. Or arguing the point that any two periods of time where I am mandated to show up and commit time to an activity that has nothing, no matter how you connect those lines and dots, to do with what I intend to be teaching this month, is, in fact, a *staff* meeting. And also physically impossible. Even better, mentally sobbing and whining over how I would much rather be spending my time planning, preparing, and getting ahead of my due dates. But how much change would be raised and how much of my precious time and energy would be wasted if I spent this time complaining? That is where I chose to reflect.

I took a look at everything and anything that I thought of or saw as my complaints, my barriers, the time-stealing tasks, and time-wasting habits; separated what was mandatory, priority, non-negotiable, and secondary; dissected my responsibilities, duties, and the stuff I just wanted to do; and analyzed the entire process as far as I had experienced it. When I took a step back and looked at what was really holding me back, I was able to separate my responsibilities and duties as a teacher into two major headers: things within my realm of control and the things that were completely outside of it.

Most of the scenarios I mentioned prior were examples of things out of my control. Emails still come, students with caseworkers and specifications still come, and staff, committee, and team meetings will continue to require your time. Unscheduled mandatory events and instances can occur simultaneously at any instant. That is just an unchangeable reality of the job. The other things are things that I wouldn't be able to change if I just continued to complain about them.

I knew these complaints had a lot to do with what I refer to as the backend or the other side of teaching, the actual workload, the work involved outside of student behaviors and managing a classroom)\. When I first began teaching, I expected some tasks to be tedious and more time-consuming than others. I wasn't surprised to have meetings and spend time planning and prepping, but I did not expect to spend my entire life doing so.

Even beyond the grading of papers, there are insane requirements for productivity and immediate response expected in addition to your planning and instructing, as well as the constant professional projects we are expected to be enthusiastic about and contribute to. Those alone are almost a second full-time researcher and analyst job in themselves. The worst part is, oftentimes, an enormous amount of effort and expectation are put forth towards these tasks in the beginning, but somewhere along the middle they fade out and completely die by the end. You end up spending so much effort and time for nothing at all. Or at least, not even to be mentioned again for fear that administration may suddenly decide, "Yeah, let's just finish that one project out for the sake of data and accolade."

I categorized my biggest hurdles into three main groups: productivity, paperwork, and people communication and interactions. These were the obstacles that kept me from being able to complete my priority tasks and produce the outcomes that I needed to achieve. For me, that job was done by 4:15 p.m., fifteen minutes just past the bell time.

SO MUCH TO DO, SO LITTLE TIME

The amount of time given throughout the school day for an elementary school teacher is generally broken into thirty-minute segments between specials and the end of the day. This can truly suck when you are trying to mentally map things out in your mind and you don't have much time to do so – not to mention part of this planning has to include using the restroom because you're a teacher and when else do you get to use the restroom?

Too often, we find ourselves spending our entire planning period *planning* what it is that we want to do. By the time we get to actual planning, you have seven minutes until student pickup. I know how frustrating it feels to, time and time again, run into the same problem in various ways: someone stopping me in the hallway for a quick conversation, or me wandering my classroom and organizing something ridiculous or severely low on the priority scale, just so I could feel like I was being productive. When I had had enough, I decided if all else failed, I would just grade. There is always grading to do, and I can always do everything else after school, right? Wrong.

After the first few years of taking your work home every day, you may still have the habit of packing the bag and taking it home, but you certainly are not doing the work. At least I wasn't. Those days were intentionally over for me. So that just left time after school, but the truth was the time after school was not always guaranteed. More importantly, it's the end of a day of teaching, which meant being mentally fried. Who wants to jump into an intensive planning session or data analysis after you have given 110% of yourself to at least thirty (in my case eighty-four) individuals on a nonstop basis for the last six hours? Not me, for sure. I'd rather do something lighter like room wandering – cough, cough – I mean organizing.

That's when I began to realize; planning my day according to my level of energy and the degree of priority made really good sense. When it came to establishing my productivity, I had to be realistic and sensible to the one who would be completing the tasks – *me*.

My first experiences were rocky. There were a few obstacles, but I made it through. More than that; I picked up a few gems along the way too. My purpose for this book is to share with you my journey: what I gained and learned that helped me to overcome these obstacles. Join me on this ride, and let's leave the stressors that overwhelm behind as you successfully navigate your day-to-day work and ultimately rediscover the joys of teaching.

CHAPTER 2

CHAPTER 2

"I Teach, We Teach, Are We All Failing Together?"

Journal Entry from August 2015:

"What I must remember is to breathe, relax, find calm, and trust God. I am going to be circulating more people this year. I must remember to prime my ears and mind my tongue. I don't want to be a gossip nor fall into the realm of "flock mentality."

I want to shine and improve, show myself, her growth, our growth. I do not want to allow myself to fall victim to mediocracy. I am ready to prove myself.

Love always,
Danielle"

I wrote that just before the school year had begun. It was my third year in fifth grade, and I would no longer be self-contained. My principal gave us the option of departmentalizing our grades into three- and two-teacher teams. I had the option of joining the three-member team and becoming a science and social studies teacher only. The opportunity was a dream. No longer would I have to be responsible for planning, prepping, and grading for six subjects. I would now only be responsi-

ble for two. Two! Are you kidding me? This also included the added bonus of already enjoying the members of my soon-to-be team. What a dream!

I said yes without hesitation. I knew that a three-member team meant more classes, but it also meant that I might finally have the opportunity to live the dream I had envisioned for myself when I became a teacher. I wanted to be able to teach well, love my job, and go home. Sure, I knew from time to time some things may need to be taken home to be reviewed or developed. Sure, I was all for the idea, if it was from time to time – not the reality of that happening every single day and most weekends too. When the reality hit me, let's just say the dream began to differ – significantly.

That reality had hit me several times over. Prior to being hired as an elementary fifth-grade teacher, I took a long-term substitute position as a first-grade teacher in the middle of the school year. It was a class-room-takeover position I was eager to have and supposed to assume from February until the end of the school year in June. It also came with the added promise of a "guaranteed" fulltime hire in the position of my choice at that school the following year.

For a young, ambitious, and naive fresh-out-of-college graduate like myself, the opportunity was ideal. I went in for an interview on Thursday and agreed to begin working the following Monday. It was one of the swiftest hiring processes I had been through. That should have been a red flag for me right there, but it wasn't. I had optimistically convinced myself, "Of course it worked out; it was meant to be!" Ideally, I was not wrong. The position afforded me the experiences that would ultimately enable me to produce the blueprint to the teaching frameworks to not only help me survive but thrive. At the end, that made it completely worth it.

Wait, let me back up a bit and share with you why I said yes to the above position so quickly.

My first-year experience was awful if I am being honest. On the surface, it appeared that I was doing a phenomenal job. My students were excelling; the classroom was well managed. When you walked into the room, there was teaching and learning and student engagement. You could see visible evidence of a teacher's hard work and evident payoff of student achievement and progress all over the walls and students' faces. But what you didn't see, consumed by student elation and good news, was the look of pure exhaustion and strain of stress on the teacher, struggling just to turn the page.

I was that teacher. My unofficial first year first-grade experience was unbelievable. Imagine the first experience anywhere as a new teacher. Then subtract the whole first half of the year, getting to know your students, and growing with the curriculum phase because you've been dropped in the middle of the school year just before spring. If that wasn't enough of a doozy on its own, the school had a new principal, and she was not well received, to say the least. She had new ideas and a new manner in which to go about them that did not include staff opinion or seem to mind staff protest. "I'd like to remind you to refer to the contract you signed…" was one of her often-used staff meeting openers.

She was the contractually-my-way type and I, at that time, was the ambitiously-my-way type. We both had a head and heart for the "there is no stopping me" and the "I can do anything" mentality, and she saw it right away. I mentioned it was a quick hire but a very comfortable and authentic interview. She expressed her immediate need for a teacher and her high expectations. I expressed my immediate interest in a teaching position and my high expectations as well. Our connection was instant, and it remained throughout the time I was teaching in first grade. Right up until the Monday I reminded her, after giving weeks in advance notice, that that Friday was going to be my last. She was shocked and could not believe it. I believe I remember her saying something like, "Oh, yes, I remember we talked about that. We discussed it. But I thought everything was solved. You seemed fine; you weren't complaining anymore."

I resented that final remark but could take my joy in knowing no matter what, that Friday would be my final and last day in that place ever again. No matter what she asked, demanded, or assumed, after Friday, I would not be working for her.

She somehow was remised of the weeks prior when I said to her that I was having a hard time and I would no longer be working there after spring break. "I will no longer be working here after spring break." That was the bit of information she seemingly overlooked. She held onto "I am having a hard time," and based on that, she jumped into quick-fix mode and took one subject away for my classroom paraprofessional to teach. It was a lovely, temporary solution to my pressing problem. I accepted that offer but wisely did not allow that help to sway my decision. And here is why: while the paraprofessional did his best, he was a paraprofessional and not a teacher. He still needed help and guidance. Even if it was first-grade math, the students were impacted.

Regardless, I was thankful to have one less lesson to plan for. I could focus on the other five, as well as all the other responsibilities – classroom, teacher, paperwork, meetings and of course, grading and feedback, parent emails, email emails, assessing data.

I in no way want it to sound like I was not grateful for the relief in load. It just was not enough to convince me to stay. The comparison was something like that of a mother preparing Thanksgiving dinner and décor before the family arrives and someone offering to bake the bread and buy the wine. Thank you, those things are important, but in order to do at least half of those things, you had to be in the kitchen and/or in the way to do them.

To be fair, before the conversation about having a hard time and leaving was the conversation about having a hard time and needing help. In response, I was supplied with a task force of people to meet with each day after school to aid in the planning and all things that instructionally we *thought* I needed help in. The reality was almost every afternoon of the week – except Friday because teachers like to go home on Fridays – was spent meeting with someone. Whether it was productive or unproductive, all of my time was spent under the narrative and influence of someone else. This would not have been a bad thing if I still was not going home and spending the remaining six hours of my day before midnight planning, writing lesson plans, grading papers, and trying to prepare or catch up to be prepared for the days ahead. I felt like I was constantly planning and preparing to plan to have some free time, but I never could get to it. There was always something more important, more pressing, a priority waiting to be addressed.

The most insane part about it all was that I was addressing them. I actually was taking it upon myself to address – promptly, might I add – all of those pending matters and priorities. I made the mistake of pursuing what my ideal vision of the super teacher was – great. On top of everything, effortlessly great. That's who I was pursuing.

On the surface, it appeared that I was doing wonderfully. According to all the dots and lines of what it "looks" to be a really good teacher, I was her. I developed great lessons that were rigorous and challenging yet engaging and creative. They were detailed and met the assessment standards being evaluated. Students had begun to make gains in their reading, and data showed an increase in math fluency. Academic engagement and participation had increased. Students not only appeared to be but were actually making all-around progress.

My classroom management appeared to be sound and in tiptop shape because it was.

This is something I have always believed to be key in successfully and safely operating a classroom. Classroom management is a very present and forward thing. You cannot get past it. It's the first thing people see and one of the first things they judge you on as well. It is also one of the first obstacles and can be the hardest. But being a born achiever and superstar teacher, classroom management thankfully wasn't a thing for me. I relied on that and was sure once I got the classroom under control, the teaching and planning would all come together.

In addition to being an ambitious achiever, I also had a pretty big ego. Teaching was something that came naturally to me and something that I believe I was destined to do. I never questioned "how" or "if" I would; it was always "I am going to be a teacher." Although I do believe destiny had plans for me and teaching, a significant part of that "I am" belonged to my ego.

One of my biggest flaws was ego and believing that it was guaranteed that I would be great at teaching and that I could do it all by myself. I not only had to look like I was the best. I actually had to be the best – the super-est super teacher, the best scores, the best line walking down the hallway, the best attendance, and when I could make it happen, the best boards in the hall. "Congratulations Miss Felton" and "Congratulations to Miss Felton's class" were things I certainly strived to hear. I mean, who would strive to be the worst or the most average, right? I also loved and had an incredible passion for what I was doing. I had just graduated from college and was young, fresh, and ready.

I had the outfits, the fancy sleek work bag, the lunch box, and a killer smile to go with it. My professionalism, pedagogy, and discourse were still fresh and on point. To anybody looking at me from the outside, I was thriving and unbothered. Even when I said I needed help, I would be received then quickly patted and dismissed with a badge of trustworthiness and belief: "You've got this." I can look back now and say that to my credit, many were not dismissing me. They truly did see the potential and success already in me for what I was asking for.

However, I really did not need help writing or planning lessons, besides learning the district formatting and gaining some wonderful strategies and resourceful tips for strengthening and adding rigor. I needed help with my lesson planning and development, but I did not know where it was that I actually needed to be helped. Ultimately, time after time, again and again, I was not asking for the help I needed and receiving exactly that.

I was grateful for the willingness of help and, oftentimes, the ear to listen but was so frustrated at the lack of resolve. I would look in classrooms and see teachers sitting at their desks with papers they were reviewing or possibly planning. I would look across the hall and see my teammate on his laptop or working productively around his room. Through my strained eyes, they looked peaceful, content, and perfect. Wow – how did they have the time to plan at school, grade papers at school, or do something 'fun' during their planning time that brought them joy around the classroom? Where did they find the time to actually get things done? I felt like I was always just doing things or adding them to my list to get done. When did they actually get done? Did "done" exist for me?

I needed help managing all the paperwork, meetings, appointments, and lesson planning I was expected to do each day in addition to the regular requirements for each week, not with how to plan a lesson, make a rubric, or set up some online resource or classroom. I spent hours and hours going over and sitting through information I already knew because I did not know how to ask the right questions to get help. I wanted to say, "Help me maximize my time and get things done. Help me actually eat my lunch without the urgency to go make a copy 'real quick.' Help me physically transition between unpacking and packing up materials while opening and closing a lesson. *Help me.*"

Then one day I learned that most do not have the answer. The majority of teachers do a combination or one of these three things:

1. They skip it entirely. Some stuff just does not get considered and if it does get considered it is not assessed.
2. They clock out and try their very best to do everything and give what they can until the timer runs out.
3. They prioritize, cross-curriculum when opportunities allow, and maximize their impact.

All in all, what I found is that no matter what the route, some things do not get done no matter the effort.

My underlying problem nobody could see was the hours I was up all night working on lesson plans or trying to catch up with grading. My problem was the weekends spent putting in legitimate work hours just to feel like I had accomplished something or at least gotten myself a few days ahead in the next week. What wasn't obvious was how little sleep I was getting and how little time there was for myself to rest or reflect. I was spending little to no time with family or investing in relationships or personal interests. I had friends I hadn't seen in months because I never had any time and a relationship that went from being a college romance and "Hey, I need a couple of hours to prep for an exam," to "Sorry babe, I'm busy teaching, grading, planning, working. In fact, are you free? Do you want to come over and grade some papers?"

I can still vividly remember the Saturday morning I set my alarm to wake up at 7:30 a.m. because I did not want to waste any of my day not knocking out work. I woke up, grabbed my teacher bag, and within the half hour, my bedroom was completely covered with papers, folders stuffed with papers to grade, binders bound with curriculum, teacher and curriculum planners with papers and sticky notes falling out of them. I remember trying to jump right into working, and initially, I did. I was thrilled to be doing what I thought was a great thing getting me ahead in my work. But then suddenly, I got sick to my stomach. I could not believe it. Why was life suddenly literally all about school and paperwork? I spent far more time consumed in work than I did actually teaching, living, or eating combined.

I remember when the movie *Bad Teacher* came out with Cameron Diaz. I said to myself no matter what, I can afford to stop and watch a movie this Saturday. At least I can say that I did something I haven't done literally since the day I started working this job.

If you've ever seen the movie, you know the plot and how it goes. The fact that Diaz is a teacher is more of a character trait and circumstance than a job, but it did give me a few good laughs, and it was a cool few moments of time free of *almost* everything to do with teaching.

For me though, I suppose my biggest comparisons came from looking at Diaz's character, who was a not so good, lazy, and pretty unenthused teacher and the character played by Lucy Punch, who was an overachieving, superstar, super passionate super teacher.

Diaz's character initially represented, for me, everything I never wanted to become: a laissez-faire, burnt-out, job-hating, check-collecting teacher.

While I was disgusted with her work ethic, I did admire her 'non' teacher attitude, and I loved her style. Punch's character, on the surface, resembled a lot of whom I wanted to be like as a teacher with a supreme commitment and exceptional work ethics. But I loathed her style and found her character to be a bit obnoxious. On a superficial surface, Diaz was one end of the spectrum, completely free, enjoying her life and failing at teaching, and Punch was on the other.

While portrayed as all smiles and butterflies, the reality of Miss Punch's life is probably, obviously, very little time committed to her personal life because she's spending most of her evenings planning, plotting, and prepping for school. That rash and hives outbreak she got from poison ivy would really have been a rash and hive outbreak from anxiety and panic attacks. The nights she spent stressing about Timberlake would be equally matched and raised by the nights spent stressing about the forest of paperwork she feels like she's drowning in from work.

That was my first-grade experience. When I went back into teaching officially as a fifth-grade teacher two years later, I had a better handle on myself and what I was going to allow. But I was still swimming in a pile of paperwork, never reaching my task, completing and traveling back and forth with a teacher rolling bag that resembled a suitcase.

There was one time when one of my nosy students claimed to have dropped their pencil just so that they could see what was behind my desk. When he saw the rolling bag I had tucked away underneath my desk, he jumped up and asked, "Miss Felton, do you live here?" I was so caught off guard, I couldn't help but start laughing. I knew right then I had to let the rolling bag go. I did eventually, but that did not stop me from still being the bag lady and bringing things home each night and the weekends too for years to come.

Now let's connect the dots and bring everything up to speed. Fast forward to where we started, the idea of having only two subjects to plan for was a dream. In my mind, this meant I would finally be able to get back to the dream and live it! Having to manage two more classes would have its challenges, but that would be minor in comparison to my previous assignment. That was what I thought.

So, I jumped right in, and the following school year, I was teaching my first year as a fifth-grade science and social studies teacher. I was partially right about my joy. It was much nicer having to plan for only two subjects. Having to manage three classes was more on the work-load, as expected, but not much more than I expected. The fact that my curriculums would be changing each year for the next three years? Well, that was the unexpected part.

I was back to where I had come from. It wasn't taking me six hours each night, but it was still constantly taking up at least two, and some of my weekends too.

Halfway through the year, I had enough. Things were going to change for me. After January, I would not be taking a workbag home back and forth each day. I would designate my days. I would not be spending crazy hours after school or getting up at the crack of dawn to put in crazy half hours before school. I would not have homework on the weekends except for Sunday evening work prep. I was done.

My biggest problems were how to manage my time and my work-load. Nobody ever talked about that. Everybody always said, "Well, y'all know, teachers have a lot of work to do." Yes, but *how*? How do I plan and build a lesson in an hour while also changing objectives, updating boards, and changing out center manipulatives? Thankfully, all these things seemed to get done, but at what cost? For me, it almost cost my sanity and peace of mind, and definitely, my time – time with family, friends, loved ones, myself.

When I looked at my teacher-neighbors, on the right, I saw a collection of people who were indifferent or had accepted these terms. On the other side, I saw a population of people that did not subscribe to the 'teacher stress' or complaint culture. They had somehow figured out the secret, the secret to teaching, being a good teacher, enjoying their job, and going home. This was the secret society of teachers that traveled over the weekends and still arrived early and with a smile for work on Monday. They went to the beach or out to dinner on a Wednesday evening just because. "Oh yeah, sorry for the yawn, caught a concert last night with my spouse." You did what? On a school night? I could only wish. I didn't see them at the copier twelve times a day, four days a week, and right or wrong, they always just seemed to have the "best" classes too. What was their secret, and why did the refuse to share it?

I'd even been brave enough to ask a few once or twice and the response always seemed to be the same. Taken more so as a compliment, they gave a humbled "thank you," and maybe a tip or strategy. I came to realize either the secret was "top secret" and wasn't going to be shared or that they didn't know the secret. It was just their outcome, their choice in how to spend their time serving this career.

That was the secret. It was a choice. They chose not to subscribe to common thought. Being stressed to the maximum was a culture of teaching I could not find myself committing to. That was not going to be me. I was going to have to find some way to be comfortable with not being the absolute best while still being able to do my best.

Whether they were going to share their individual secrets to managing workloads and maintaining work passion or could not explain them, it didn't matter anymore. I knew what the secret was, and I was making the choice to not subscribe to personal chaos too.

I was able to separate my duties as a teacher into individual duty categories: the teacher who teaches and is immersed in student and classroom culture; the teacher who teaches and directly interacts with the students and provides the instruction; the teacher who knows the teaching, information, and prep work required to teach and the materials and resources necessary to facilitate instruction. Grading papers is a part of the teaching requirements because we should be grading things with the purpose of informing our instruction and/or student value.

Then there's the professional educator who primarily deals with paper and adults. The professional portion of the job has the greatest responsibilities. A large part of the professional side of teaching involves the sciences – the social sciences, educational sciences, behavioral sciences, interpersonal interactions, and caseload management. It includes the meetings and action research, district objectives and the learning targets, school missions and improvement plans. The other side includes showing up to work and picking up students on time, abiding by the additional set of rules outlined in the staff handbook, showing up to duty posts, writing incident reports whenever any incident occurs, reporting, following up and trailing an incident. Writing reports and documenting documentation of such are also a part of the professional requirements.

From the duty categories, there are sub-columns divided into responsibilities and requirements. For each sub-column, identify the tasks, time and tools necessary to complete for the duty category.

I took this challenge in three parts: the physical,(the external 'needs'), the internal 'orders,' and the inter-social/personal. The physical aspect is things that physically relate to classroom function and daily life. What are the responsibilities that I am physically responsible for within the classroom on a routine basis? For me, classroom changeover was my first task. I needed to take a look at how I could either relieve myself of the duty or complete it in a way that was quick and easy each day. The classroom changeover tasks included things like the monthly calendar, adding feedback to the student work, adding work to the student work board, manipulatives, and changing centers. I found that all these tasks were jobs that students could take on – with structure and proper guidelines.

Daily classroom duties such as the board and changing the objectives, copies, collecting work, distribution of work, and the teaching were things that I would have to do. Planning, lesson building, unpacking of curriculum, preparing of content, and gathering resources were also things I would have to do. Being able to do them in the time that I was given, efficiently and completely, was my goal. So I had better figure out how to manage them because there was nowhere to hide.

The second obstacle was the internal 'orders,' a.k.a. the paperwork. I used the term internal 'orders' partly to be dramatic and also to emphasize the 'orders.' If you do not discern and prioritize, the paper aspect of teaching can and will become your true master. The paperwork, the

deadlines, the dues – 'the orders.' Some of these orders include grading papers, creating the papers to grade, rubrics, caseloads and tracking student information. The paperwork phase describes anything that is done or having to do with paper. In the classroom, that is a lot of things. There is no getting around it. You can do things online or limit your printouts, but the outcomes that come from the paperwork are still going to remain. So, I had to find a way to again be productive and manage my time in a way that effectively prioritized the paperwork that had to be done and was postponing the rest.

The third was inter-social/personal interactions. This is people and communication management. As a teacher, you are always talking to someone. There is an endless array of interactions that occur through-out the day, and each one can be drastically different. It is important to know how to navigate, negotiate, and decipher such situations because you never know what you might walk into on a seemingly completely normal day.

Teaching has been one of my greatest challenges and greatest adven-tures. Each day is an opportunity for either to surface in positive or negative ways. Narrowing down the three main contenders – what stopped me productively, paperwork that overwhelmed me, and managing people communication in a way that is timely and bares good results – was key in my ability to develop the systems and rou-tines that allowed me to successfully negotiate each day with simplic-ity and sophistication.

CHAPTER 3

CHAPTER 3

"Objectives, Please"
– A Framework and Overview

G ood morning and good greetings to you, Dear Teacher! I am so happy and so glad you have made it here. If you have made it this far, you've read past my story and found yours somewhere between the lines. I am happy to have met you. The remainder of this book will be completely for you. Let us begin with an objective!

OBJECTIVE

Today you will be introduced to *Teach and Go Home!* But this is not your ordinary teacher's book – this book is different. Would you like to know how? It is a story about a teacher who discovered the secret superpowers of optimizing and simplifying their workload so they would be able to teach and go home. (Pause and deeply inhale for dramatic effect.)

"But what does that mean, teach and go home?" asks a scholar who did not raise their hand.

"Yeah, what about homework?" says another.

"What about studying and my academic success scores? How do I do manage those?" asks one more, both without a hand.

Yes, all great questions. Today we will find out exactly what all that means.

INTRODUCTION

In the following chapters, you will be introduced to the frameworks and outlines for how to manage your workload and, frankly, get back to *teaching*, your joy, your passion – ultimately get back to you! These systems are designed for organizing the "teaching tower of to-dos" ffec-tively, efficiently, and with little effort beyond the action you have to put in to complete it. In addition, the teacher tendencies in me could not resist a few catchy phrases and acronyms to remember some of these too. To set a tone for common understanding, we will introduce some of your key vocabulary and important terms for this lesson.

OUR KEY VOCABULARY

- Teacher – n. v. adj. sb. (supreme being) – a practical superhero. They are required to face oppositions, encounter obstacles, and be tested in physical endurance and emotional strength.

  A teacher describes what it means to be devoted to, sacrifice for, and serve others for the greater good of the future. Everything a teacher is is for the development and improvement of someone else's ability to succeed. To be a teacher is to be duality, to be both concrete and abstract, flexible and structured, first and last, right and wrong.

- Sophisticate(d)(cation) – n. v. – this describes that extra touch of flair or style, the quality or attention to detail you have, the manner of professionalism, your splash of fun or excitement, etc.; it is the distinguishing factor that I describe as 'sophistication.'

What is your distinguishing and sophisticated touch? For me, I would say that people may first assume that mine is style. They would not be completely wrong, but it is not a fashion style; it is an 'era' style. I'm traveling somewhere behind Mary Poppins and Phylicia Rashad's closet and expectations, carrying a torch for professionalism etiquette. I fell in love with the stern, passionate, loving, no-challenge-too-great high expectations, along with the high-waisted A-line skirts, brim-collared shirts, and ties style and demeanor of my former teachers. My favorite and usually toughest teachers always carried their own versions of sophisticated professionalism. They did not all dress in a dress shirt or skirts, but they all carried that attitude. To sophisticate or add sophistication simply means to take an already lovely process and enhance or improve that process with your own confidence and distinguishing quality.

- Simplify(ing)(ied) – v. n. – this term does not mean a shortcut. To simplify means to find the shorter and/or most efficient and effective route.

  For this definition, I have prepared an example.

  Topic: Chopping Garlic

  ◊ Example One: I brought a garlic press to simplify my process of chopping garlic, but it can only hold a couple of cloves at a time and can't go in the dishwasher. I have to hand wash it, and it's hard to get into the crevices to clean them.

  ◊ Example Two: I first peel the flower skins and chop the rough ends off all the garlic I will need. Then I grab a rubber mallet

and a damp paper towel to cup the garlic and protect the mallet. I mash the garlic cloves to my desire and grab a knife to rough chop the garlic finely. Finally, I use the opposite side of the paper towel to wipe up any stray pieces and the mallet if necessary. I will put the knife in the dishwasher when I am finished using it. Garlic chopping and clean-up are complete. I continue cooking.

My start may take me a be a bit longer, but once I have finished, I am done, and the task is complete. Those two differences in simplifying alone can make or break the overall time spent productively or wastefully into completing tasks.

Of all the things mentioned in this entire book, these two terms alone may be the most meaningful and important things to me – PPOP and PIG. If nothing else, please walk away knowing what it means to do these two things. These two terms will be essential and oftentimes unspoken frameworks for which you will begin to operate. For now, let's just identify and discover what the letters mean. How to apply them and when will be discussed later.

The term PPOP represents the system of being Prepared, Planned, Organized, and Productive in your pursuits. The term PIG refers to the process of taking time to establish the Purpose, Intention, and Goal before you begin.

MIDWAY CHECK-IN AND EXPANSION

First, we will address and tackle some of our most necessary obstacles like the classroom and planning. In the next chapter, you will be asked to assess your own classroom design layout, challenge its organization and functionality, and learn why you should establish your own "classroom flow." I discuss a design method for unpacking and setting up your classroom that focuses on efficiency in design. It's important to have a classroom that is conducive to the daily routines and tailored to its use. Who wants a classroom that looks fantastic but nothing is ever used beyond the seats? Classrooms for show or classrooms that are serving as storage are not conducive to a productive work environment. It also does not help productivity when you a shuffling through mass amounts of unnecessary 'stuff.' Things are always falling out and hard to put back, being trampled over, or worse, you don't even know what you have.

Once we tackle the classroom, we must discuss the process of actual teaching, what it takes to prepare, and managing the workload associated with it in Chapter 5.

Later, we will get into setting personal standards and why boundaries for yourself in your profession are exceptionally good things. The significance of home/work/life balance and how to negotiate the patterns and people of your day-to-day work life will be discussed in Chapter 7. We will take the time to discuss the things they did not teach you in undergrad and don't offer at any professional development, even though they are some of the biggest barriers and time consumers we face as teachers day to day.

We complain, we overcome, and we navigate. We all are faced with the compromises that come from balancing life, work, and sanity. Yet few of us share with each other the secrets and skills they use to beat their obstacles and conquer their time-devouring monsters. Even fewer have taken the time to put that into a compressive framework. Well, here you go. I wrote this for you, dear teacher: a reference guide and resource I hope you will use, share, and refer to time and time again, the guide to simplified and sophisticated teaching, with efficiency, practicality, and sanity.

EVALUATION AND CLOSURE

As you continue through the remainder of this book, there are a few things to keep in mind. If absolutely nothing else, remember to think of the PIG before you begin. If you outline your process with PPOP, you will streamline your results. These next two are my favorites. Simplify your routines where you can, but simplification does not guarantee fast. Don't cheat yourself, and remember that sophistication is what you make it.

Along the way, you'll also find "apple bites" – these nutritional nuggets are bites of information, suggestions, and quick tips.

Here are also some ideal materials to have as you read:

- Personal materials: a beverage of your choice for sipping and enjoying the stories you will find interwoven throughout and a journal or notepad for jotting tips down!

- Professional materials: an array of felt-tip, colored non-bleed pens, a coordinating array of highlighters, a pencil with a non-smearing eraser, and colored star stickers. Place a star on pages you want to reference or share later. You can coordinate pen, highlighter and star colors to significance or category or skip the whole thing and just have fun.

You can read this book from beginning to end or jump right into the chapters you need. This is a resource, a guide, and a compilation of a few good stories too. Enjoy!

CHAPTER 4

CHAPTER 4

"Class Begins"

–PPOP Classroom: How to Structure a Simplified Functionality and Design

The classroom is not *yours;* it is theirs – the students', the ones whose learning you are facilitating. The classroom is a learning environment. Never become so attached that you could not just walk away with your bag and a box of memories. There should be nothing so valuable or personal that you would be obligated to turn back or keep locked away. In a nutshell, keep your classroom simple and to the point.

I watched *Working Girl* when I was a young girl, and that last scene when Tess walks out of Weaver's office with her box and her purse left an impression on me I will never erase. Leave with class. Leave with pride. Leave with all your items easily collected in a file box. Lightweight.

My ideal classroom is well-organized, minimalistic to a *teacher's manner,* diverse, functional, self-sufficient, and attractive. It is clean, and there is an obvious and easy way to jump into the routine and designation for important and most used items.

But first, preschool.

Before we begin, let's take a moment to meet the PIG in the room. In any and all things that you do, be sure to reference PIG before you do them. What is my classroom's purpose? What are my intentions or intended outcomes? What goal or goals have I set for myself to know when it has been achieved? Purpose, Intention, and Goal. Oink, baby, oink.

When we PIG, we are better able to PPOP efficiently. It is easier to plan and prepare organized and productively because we know what, why, and when we have done whatever it is we set out to do. It is something most of us are already doing naturally. Alrighty, we've got that down. In all that we do, we PIG. As you read through this chapter and then begin on your own, remember to PIG out before you PPOP!

THE SOPHISTICATED TEACHER'S UNPACK AND SETUP

The first week returning to school is usually a preservice week where teachers and staff are given several days to debrief, meet, and prepare their classrooms and school for the incoming students, who are usually arriving the following week. Do not be alarmed if the majority of your time seems to be spent at meetings and delegated to tasks that have nothing to do with unpacking or creating a functional learning space for incoming students.

You will be able to complete the job. You may have to dedicate additional hours. If you need to, designate a time maximum for those hours and include time spent in transportation and shopping for items. This will allow you to maximize your time and leave room for unexpected responsibilities and planning. I have had enough experience to know that the first few days *can* be enough time, but you truly have to use them strategically.

Hopefully, if you are a new teacher, you will be given an opportunity to have a spending balance for purchasing classroom items. Be informed that items purchased on the school or district account belong to the school or district. To make it easy, keep a copy of all receipts no matter how old or for how long and be sure to label each item accordingly as they come in. Labeling ideas include simply adding the school initials and room number.

When you do your room shopping personally with your own accounts, be sure to label all items accordingly with your name and keep a copy of all receipts on file until departure. When purchasing or bringing in items into the classroom that have not been funded or provided by the school – which if you truly would like a harmonious and fluid teaching life, you will – try to consider each item as a purposeful item for the classroom. Don't think about wanting it back or taking it with you if you ever leave your classroom position, unless it would truly benefit your new position. To keep it simple, rarely – and I mean extraordinarily rarely – bring personal items into the classroom that if left behind, you would be devastated over.

If they don't give you a budget, do not worry. Through my experience, I have also found that if you can let go of the "ideal" idea and make "ideal" use out of what you do have, the rest will come. You will make it yourself, or find you don't need it along the way. Most if not

all of the things that you will most need will be provided or find their way through donations to you.

Setting up and decorating your classroom is a part of all teacher's dream, customizing and laminating labels and clever posters, centers here and self-selected centers there. Oh, how colorful and filled the dreams are of a teacher and their soon-to-be classroom. At least I know that mine were.

But my dreams were not filled with award-winning customized Pinterest designed layouts or "A Kinder Town's" dream of elementary school. My classroom dreams where dreams of functionality, fluidity, and student-maintained and managed centers. They were indeed filled with bright colors and elaborate themes but not ahead of practicality and functionality or my budget.

In my first experience opening a classroom, I began with next to nothing. Literally next to nothing. Thankfully, before I opened my first classroom, I had the opportunity to teach summer school in another district. When the summer was over, all staff was free to take any left-over materials. Prior to that, I taught at another school in the same district, at the same grade level for six months and was able to obtain a few curriculum and instructional items before I left there as well. Some were parting gifts; others were overflow of classroom clutter.

The full list of entry items for my first day opening my very first classroom consisted of two bags' worth of cleaning supplies, a small group's worth of art supplies, and a box I could carry filled with bags full of unnecessary knick-knacks from the teacher store, which later proved to be completely unnecessary. No posters to decorate my walls with, no creative owl-themed banners and name tags. At first, I will admit for a moment, it did feel overwhelming to have to think of how to set up an elementary classroom with nothing after the desk and chairs. Thankfully, my school was one that did not place its priorities in decor or level of classroom cuteness. Student work and evidence of curriculum standards and student learning were more important.

Nevertheless, you will find as I did, that it will not matter how little or how much you walk into a new classroom with. As a new teacher, even if you are an old teacher, people are going to volunteer a multitude of stuff. Any time a "new" person walks in and is going to be occupying a classroom, or any space honestly, for the first time, other people come bringing baskets and stacks of both useful and not useful junk. I took everything, said thank you, and then tossed the stuff I didn't want politely into the recycle during one of my seasonal or module clean-outs.

I ended up with more things than I knew what to do with. I had more than enough baskets, containers, borders, posters from the 1980s, and patty-whacks than I knew what to do with. There was very little I needed to buy if I could accept the mixed and matched unofficial theme. I humbly accepted with immense gratitude and worked with it, scratching my Pinterest dreams for efficiency and my reality. The first classroom's official theme was exploration and learning through growth. I made a big paper tree that stretched across one of the walls with a star-filled sky that spread into the window well. That was it, and that would be us – growth, discovery, and environment. After that centerpiece and the collection of 'all types' of useful things, I didn't need anything fancy. No matter where you went, you would find something different, academic, and fun or challenging from the next corner.

The classroom is all about the students anyway. I could forgo the cute themes and cutest classroom design award for now or at least until my budget said something different.

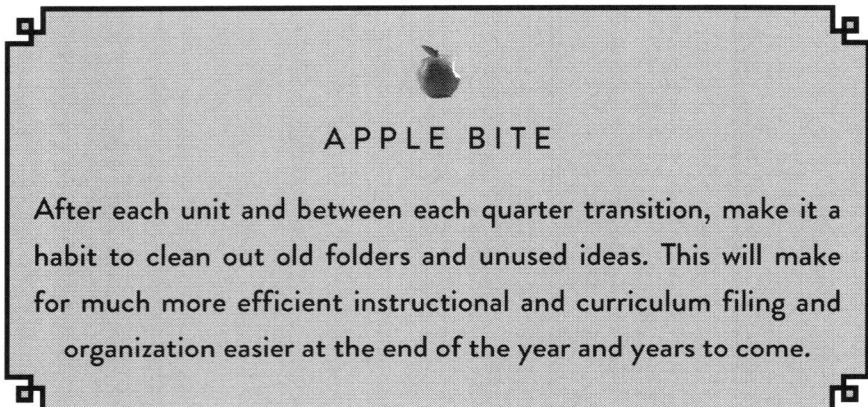

APPLE BITE

After each unit and between each quarter transition, make it a habit to clean out old folders and unused ideas. This will make for much more efficient instructional and curriculum filing and organization easier at the end of the year and years to come.

HOW TO PPOP UNPACK AND SET UP

Arrival can be overwhelming. Before you enter your classroom, enter the room with a plan and a method for your unpacking and setting up. If you are not a new teacher, hopefully, you packed up the room neatly and efficiently to make the unpacking process all the smoother. Nevertheless, by breaking the task up into steps or layers as I like to imagine, you can gradually prepare and set up your classroom with ease and hopefully with a lot less time wasted backtracking and going in circles.

This segment will be broken up into two parts. The first part is an informative section about the type of classroom unpackers and set-upers I have noticed over my years. The second part is the layers of setting up your classroom. Get yourself a good and reliable timer, easy to use and visible because you will be using it often, and a jug of water!

TYPES OF UNPACKERS

Disclaimer – remember this book is a resource and a guide. The following descriptions are not critiques or criticisms; they are observations accumulated over time that I have used to improve my own practice. You may find this useful in being able to identify which beginning of the year classroom set up personality you relate to or are aspiring to change.

The first group of people is the Early Settlers. They arrive very early in the mornings to begin setting up and/or come in a few days prior to the preservice week and begin unpacking their classrooms. They usually will have some beverage in hand to accompany their t-shirt and capri pants attire. They intend to take their time, move at their own pace, and usually have a lot of detailed themes and designs to put up. This group may even typically stay late a few (or most) evenings. They turn on their music and/or talk radio and again take their time. They are finished and complete when they are completely satisfied and not before.

There is the second group, the Help Included. The Help Included group is the group that is either going to have a hoard (two or more) of family and/or friend's children volunteering (gaining service hours) to help them set up, or they are recruiting all the non-classroom staff to assist in their chaos that they must have literally thrown into a cabinet or box, slammed against the door, and taped the lid. The work ethic with this particular group is minimal and usually disorganized. Too much time is spent telling everyone what to do rather than doing it. They will get the room together, but it will not look like it until the very last minute. Even then, they may still say it isn't done.

The third group is similar to the previous in that unpacking their classrooms can look like a bit of chaos, and they may – will – be needing extra help. But this group is not so much as a help-included group as a help-needed group. They're the Hoarders. The amount of stuff and the amount of reasoning that they can present you with for why each and every item is important and necessary for that one fateful day when it may or may not be needed depending upon whether it is or is not remembered and then depending upon whether or not it can or cannot be found is pure insanity. However, when they are ready to let go or can be talked into letting something go, I have found amongst a sea of outdated trash much repurposed treasure. Never become the hoarder, but a few generous hoarding neighbors in your hallway is not always the worst thing.

In the end, this room's set up is done by the set-up date. But the continuous mountain of growing boxes is left unpacked and some unopened until post-retirement. This room never gets fully unpacked. Items come in, and they rarely leave.

The fourth group is the Worker Bee group. They come in when it is time to arrive, maybe thirty minutes to an hour before, and do their daily tasks without much fretting and minimal complaint. When they come into the building, they go into their room and unless you run across them in the hallway, a meeting, or at the copy machine, they go into their room, and you do not see them again until the clock is done and they are walking out. You might find them leaving maybe fifteen minutes to a half-hour after but not by much and not too often. This group will have their room done for welcoming on time and accept the rest as it comes. By the final day, you usually see them sitting at a desk or table somewhere planning for the coming week with water nearby.

As I made observations and progressed in my career, I determined that I wanted my preservice week and classroom unpacking to fall somewhere between the first group and the fourth group. I wanted desperately to be able to spend at least a half of a day planning and preparing for my students' arrival, but I didn't quite have the commitment to stay late or discipline to arrive hours early. I wanted to take my time and arrive on time. I wanted to be calm and collected and be satisfied because the job was done well and completely.

LAYERS OF UNPACKING AND CLASSROOM SETUP

I believed that setting up a classroom should not take an entire week, but there are so many elements and the task never seems done until the last minute, the day before the students arrive. I found myself wasting time and walking in circles. Then I realized the number of elements wasn't the issue; it was recognizing my errors and establishing a format for how to utilize my time.

I didn't want to have a ton of people offering help and needing direction when I myself was trying to figure out what I was going to do and how. But having help is a great benefit, and from experience and the observations of other great role-model teachers – whether they knew they were my role model or not – I learned to instead enter the first days slowly and accept the meeting and other professional responsibilities as professional priorities and getting the classroom and instruction ready for students as educator priorities. Each day is dedicated to a priority and responsibility in each category. Professionalism requirements will be unique to your district and each school, but the educational responsibilities may be similar in general from classroom to classroom. Break down each phase of classroom unpacking and set

up into levels or layers that make the most sense to your classroom.

The five-layer model for unpacking your classroom can be strategically completed in about three hardworking days. The first day (layer one) of classroom unpacking should be dedicated to the preparation and planning of the classroom design and functionality you will need for your students and the coming school year.

The second day is your hardest working day. This day is for organizing your classroom for the layout it will soon become. After preparations and planning your classroom, it is time for some hardcore and thoughtful manual labor with layers two and three, the layout and functionality layers. This is where you are establishing your room function, zones, and where you will place the furniture. If you really want to knock out this day and cash in on your time and efforts, complete layers two and three completely, then prep and organize for layer four the following day. This way you've knocked out some of your hardest work.

Coming into day three, it is all about the walls and décor designing – the best parts. Each day should be all about productively executing all of your hard work. Day three is for finalizing and executing just that. After these three ordered days of un-layering, the mass of your classroom will be completely unpacked and ready for set up. You can also use these models to redesign or restructure the layout you already have set in place in your classroom. Remember to take it slow. If you are restructuring, consider changes over the course of a few weeks primarily focusing on layers two and three.

LAYER ONE: ASSESSMENT AND ACCLAMATION

The first thing I do when arriving back into my classroom post-summer break is make an assessment and acclamation of the room (Layer One).

It is this step that you are hoping is the swiftest and easiest to check off the list. If not, then the remaining layers of unpacking the classroom have the potential to be frustrating and exhausting.

The first layer can be compared to a set of dominos. If done fluidly, you can complete each step simply, flowing seamlessly into one another, but if you are missing pieces or knocking over dominos before the others arrived or at the same time, you may find yourself doing a lot of backtracking across your steps.

The assessment layer of classroom unpacking can be the simplest, or it can be the beginning of what could be a road filled with potholes. The point is that you can't begin setting up and arranging your classroom if furniture and necessary materials are damaged or missing. Proceeding that, you cannot begin to unpack if you do not have the keys to unlock the cabinets. Do not be discouraged. The great thing about potholes is that with awareness, you can possibly avoid them, and eventually they are filled, optimistically thinking. Finally, and conclusively, you must set up the internet so that you can have your music during the unpack. Also, since the internet tends to provide the most complications, it is a wise idea to use the assessment layer to determine your needs and get on any repair or concerns lists sooner than later. The list tends to grow, and solutions tend to arrive along the way. Make your needs known early so that they can be addressed promptly.

Take your time in this layer. Move productively but not aggressively. These are the first steps in setting up your classroom. I make it a point to raise the blinds to let the sun's rays in and spritz the room a few times with the scent of Macintosh apples each school year beginning. I close my eyes for a second just to absorb the moment. It is like magic how

quickly a room can be unpacked from absolutely nothing to a full and completely functional classroom in five or fewer days, twenty or fewer hours total. Teachers truly have superhuman powers.

ASSESSMENT 1: CLEANLINESS AND DAMAGES SWEEP

This assessment is easy. When you first walk in, before you do much other than expressing your gratitude for another year, take a quick observant survey of the classroom. With your first scan, you are checking for a few basic and simple things. Were the floors cleaned and polished, room swept and cleaned, walls painted? Has there been any damage done to the room over the summer – flood, infestation, or any mechanical or construction done? Is there any evidence that the classroom was used any way other than expected over the summer, such as a playroom or mini daycare, storage from another, much dustier location of the building, etc.?

The second scan is for furniture and room materials. In this second survey of the room, it is a practical idea to have a copy of the room inventory list that detailed the items in the classroom from the school year prior. Hopefully, all returned or moved (materials primarily) are undamaged. A quick comparison between the inventory sheet and a tour around the classroom's present items should suffice as a full assessment and a hopeful all-clear and yes check to this task as well.

Hopefully, you find the first survey of the room to be a very swift one that includes yes, yes, and yes to the first few subjects, then a fine list of no's as you move down the checklist. Once you can check the all-clear on assessment number one, put your bags down and prepare for assessment number two.

ASSESSMENT 2: INVENTORY AND SPACE ANALYSIS

The second assessment will hopefully be as breathtakingly simple as the first in that if it is not, you will surely also find yourself in a day or two's worth of frustration. Assessment two is for planning and plotting how your room will potentially function and where you want your furniture to be placed. This assessment should be intentional and thoughtful. This is where you will spend the bulk of your mental energy in designing your room. The second assessment is where you create the vision for your room. What will each day function like? How do I want the students to be able to manipulate and circulate the classroom? Where will things go? Why am I putting them there? What is the purpose I intend to achieve? Assessment two is where you piggy, piggy, PIG for your room.

APPLE BITE

Be mindful of unpacking when packing up the classroom the year prior. If possible, store items as compact as possible in their designated setup locations for energy- and timesaving. Do not feel compelled to pack all the puzzles together in the closet if when you are going to take them down and set up your classroom you are going to put them in all different designated locations like the shelves across the room. Basically, be mindful of the classroom's design when you choose the way you pack it.

This now concludes the end of the layer one assessments. You may now progress onto the next dynamic.

I hope you got an A-plus and found your room assessments quite easy, quite simple, and quite quick. The final dynamic of unpacking your classroom is to get your room keys; typically the room door will have already been unlocked for you. Your room keys include your copy of your room key as well as the keys to the file and room cabinets. Once you unlock the cabinets, get your tech and internet cables out and set up the internet if you are not in a wireless classroom and set the tunes up!

APPLE BITE

"Cleanliness is safety too." Take a bite of wisdom, and clean as you work. The classroom should have been cleaned while you were away, but an intentional wipe-down and sweep before you work are great habits to adopt while unpacking. Sweep corners and along baseboards while you can before you move furniture into those locations. A spritz or two of disinfectant and an air-dry might benefit any rodents and six-legged friends. Give the countertops and desks a thorough wipe and air dry while you can be sure little fingers won't write their names in the formula residue as it dries. And don't forget to drench or scrub down the telephone, sink, cabinet, and door handles.

The sterilization won't last long or forever, but it will feel great, productive, and give your room a very fresh and clean start to the year.

Knowing that I have also physically come through and swept and wiped the classroom as I unpack truly does give me a sense of ownership and responsibility for the classroom, not the extreme vanity of "This is *my* classroom" but the unity to the building and the school and the learning community that will soon be fostered within the walls by taking those additional steps to really prepare and prep the room for the students.

LAYER TWO: CLASSROOM LAYOUT, FUNCTIONALITY AND WORKSTATIONS

When you first begin to set up your classroom, before you jump head-first into your heart's desires, think of your daily and weekly needs. The classroom is an extension of your instruction and an environment dedicated to safety and learning first.

You should develop a philosophy, a belief, something you hold true and stand by, and it should be short and simple. My classroom is such:

This is a classroom; this is my temporary dwelling space. It is my working space. It is not my home or my own. Therefore, I believe my classroom should have a purposeful design that is representative of a comfortable and conducive space for an academic dwelling; a.k.a., I want my classroom to also have the favoritisms of a home environment.

Your classroom design can be greatly enhanced or inhibited by the size and layout of your classroom's structure, and for that reason, we will not spend much time focusing on design at all. Instead, I would rather focus your attention on purpose, the purpose for the classroom.

Ideally, you want a classroom that's easy to access, clean, and functioning. Notice the present tense "-ing," not functional. Take it back to the first principle of the classroom – the classroom is not your own. It is a workspace, a working space. If anyone should come into the classroom to work, they should be able to take a moment in observation and identify how to operate about and immerse themselves within the classroom. Have clear and labeled locations for frequented items, such as supplies, paper, pencils, markers, glue, scissors, etc. to avoid guests having to ask the students or you to borrow simple supplies.

Another benefit of having a simple and seamless classroom is that it makes it easy for new students to identify and immerse themselves in the routines. It will also make it easier for staff and support team members that transition into the classroom to access items they need to work with students without disrupting you or other students. Keep things as simple and seamless as possible when it comes to classroom design and location of center designations.

With all of that being said, I am going to ask you to do something that may seem counterintuitive or unusual for the remainder of this stage. As we prepare our minds for this layer, I want you to think "the kitchen." We are going to use the mentality we use for preparing and setting up our personal kitchens as the metaphoric framework for the design and setup of our classroom.

Think about it; the kitchen in your home is not only the place where food is stored and produced. It also represents the heart of the home. The kitchen is for producing, creating, storing, gathering, preparing, conversing, and so much more (assuming you also eat at the kitchen table). Practically everything but sleeping and using the restroom are done in the kitchen. A similar thought can be applied to the classroom.

When we prepare our kitchens, we are preparing them with the ideas of function, location, access and usage, space and storage. We don't throw things in drawers or follow a setup plan based on someone else's kitchen. We set our kitchens up based on our routines, our habits, the resources and space we have and what we intend to be doing in it. There is an order and a logical or practical reason for everything, usually.

The thought process behind setting up a classroom is just about the same, but instead of cooking, it's teaching. Instead of a stove, you have a teaching station where you cook up learning. Just as it is important for your kitchen to have a fluid and seamless function, it is important for you as a teacher to have a classroom design that is seemless and fluid for your to work from. It is equally important, as it is in your kitchen, to have a simple and efficient design that is easy for others to access and cook in too.

We can describe our classroom kitchens comparatively into zones: the cleanliness and cleansing zone (the sink); the work, preparation, production and presentation zone (the countertops and tables around the classroom); the cooking zone (your teaching station where you present and introduce lessons from). Your pantry and cabinets for storing in your kitchen would be the cabinets, closet, and teacher task tower you have in your classroom. That desk or mini-study that few people actually sit down at in the kitchen, that can be considered the teacher desk, perspectives depending. And the student desks are your kitchen table. Everyone has a seat!

The curriculum materials are your cookbooks and the tools you use to teach with your cooking utensils. Spoon, knife, and fork; pen, highlighter, and pencil. Salt and pepper, markers and glue. The spice rack is your classroom resources that are routinely or are occasionally used like dictionaries and manipulatives. In some people's kitchens, they have a command center on a wall or on the refrigerator door where they keep household updates, important information, and the family calendar and their kids' work. Your command center and postings in the classroom are your boards. As we continue through layers two, you will be reading about my classroom kitchen and what best works for the resources and layout I have. Everyone's kitchen has its parallels, but we each utilize ours differently. These ideas are tailored to me, you will tailor your classroom design to you. Keep your kitchen in mind. Classroom kitchen, Think, kitchen-istically!

So, for this exercise, let's presume both space and resources are in accessible supply. This is not an "if I had my dream classroom" exercise; this is function, practicality, basics, and efficiency for my reality.

FUNCTION AND LAYOUT LOCATIONS

This layer of classroom unpacking is probably my favorite layer and the most important to me as the instructor. This layer is the meat and potatoes of the classroom's daily function. It should be fluid, efficient, and simple. Proper and thoughtful setup of the workstations, student and teacher planning areas, and instructing and material storage make a huge impact. This can contribute greatly to the overall function of the classroom, impacting both structure and routine, but also can contribute a significantly positive impact on the planning and instruction process for the teacher.

Part one is the classroom design and layout, which describes the basic structures or zones of your room and the perimeter zones along the edges of your classroom.

Part two is the workstations, including teacher desk, instruction stations for both whole and small group instruction, carpet and any student and other workstations around the room.

PART ONE: CLASSROOM DESIGN AND LAYOUT FUNCTIONS

◇ THE SINK

Every classroom should have a sink. Unless you are in a temporary structured dwelling, *all classrooms should have sinks*. Could you imagine a doctor's office with no sink? The thought is just frightening. In the classroom, the feelings are the same. Think about the amount of time and cleanup concocting temporary water solutions with bins and buckets. The different germs and bacteria exchanged over documents and the manipulatives alone. Sending students out or taking "class trips" to the two stalled and sink restrooms for students to wash hands and drink water, being able to wash your own hands alone is crazy without a sink. The sink is primary.

Now that we have gotten a brief preface on the importance of the classroom sink, let us begin with the setup.

I believe above all things the classroom should be safe. There should be a designated safety and cleaning area in your classroom too. The kitchen or the bathroom sink in the home is socially designated safe and 'get wet' places. Continuously, I've seen many classrooms will have a station or an area that is designated as the primary area for water and storing safety and cleaning supplies.

The PIG for the sink are safety, supplies, and water.

A practical setup would be as follows:

- First Aid, Supplies, and Cleanliness: The primary stock of band-aids, sanitizer, tissues, Ziplocs, and overflow cleaning wipes and non-bleach sprays should all be housed in this region. It is the natural reach and grab to open the sink cabinets for things of that nature.

- *A Cafe:* A practical idea is to store all things related to food and cleanliness, meaning if space allows, napkins, plasticware, paint and brushes, mugs, cleaning supplies diluted and on the highest shelf. A very small and wise idea is a simple container roll of platstic wrap or an inexpensive Tupperware set for the impromptu treats and take-home meals that sometimes come up, and you never have anything to carry the uneaten items home.

In my cabinet, I also keep a very deep large coffee mug to function as a bowl with a handle for lunches or last-minute breakfast, rarely tea. I would not encourage drinking from a container without a lid within the classroom and certainly not one with such an open and wide brim. There are a lot of curious bodies that would love to smell, examine, and talk all over your beverage if given the opportunity.

I also keep a small container of dish soap and a dish scrubbing sponge, both purchased from the dollar store for specifically quick cleaning of Tupperware and lunch containers. I don't use the items often, but when it is necessary, I am so thankful to have them easily available and on hand. A second dish-scrubbing brush in a different color and kept labeled is another great tool that is not used often, but you are so thankful to have when needed. It's a three-dollar investment into your classroom but priceless for your peace. The basic sink should be simple, functional, and not over-cluttered.

A luscious idea is a bit of seasonal decor you are not too attached to, a set of hand soap and lotion just for you and a room scent plug-in. Keeping the box of tissues next to the sanitizers isn't an *un-smart* idea, and *voila*, the sink is complete. If you have plenty of space and can ensure your sink items won't get wet, it is a good location to utilize as secondary storage.

◊ WINDOWSILLS AND COUNTERTOPS

Windowsills and countertops are for additional workstations and displays. They are not for clutter or mounds of things, although storage can be limited, and I have certainly found myself guilty of that one once or more than twice. If you have windowsills, try to leave them as neat and minimal as possible. There should not be many obstructions to the view beyond curtains or blinds, and items placed in the window should contribute an aesthetic flair to the classroom. After all, the classroom window sometimes can be one of the few opportunities to witness the actual day.

The PIG for the Windowsills: Clean, crisp, purposeful, and visually organized are attractive traits for a windowsill. An area for collecting dust, old papers, and storing miscellaneous items are not.

Within my current classroom, I have two windows along the same wall with two separate windowsills. One window is near my desk, and in this windowsill, I store a file rack, and a few instructional binders and items I access frequently during my planning process, and a plant.

The second window is located toward the center of the classroom and that is where tissues, sanitizer, and the current books I want to advertise for student use are displayed.

They serve perfectly as individual academic spaces. The locations are easy to distinguish in the room. When I am running groups or rotations, I clear that area and often use it as a designated location for accessing materials. Because it is simple and easy to clean and clear off, the area is purposeful and used often. The free space along my windowsill I often use as an area for incoming graded papers, projects, and late work. When the area gets too cluttered, I know I have gotten behind on grading a project or miscellaneous late work. Visual cues are important.

◊ CLOSETS CABINETS, AND SHELVES

Coat Closet

Think of any closets in your classroom as your pantry and storage facilities. Students should not have access to these areas. Be practical and resourceful – it is not productive to pull everything you need out each time.

PIG for Closets: If you can, use every bit of space practically, stored organized and neatly for access.

I believe in keeping your personal items to a minimum. With that in mind, I don't actually end up needing much of the space within my coat closet. The closet in my classroom is a standard closet, with one shelf and a metal rod to hold hangers. I use that space to hold two hangers, one that is constantly occupied with an old sweater and scarf in case I catch an emergency chill or if an extra layer is needed for recess duty. The second hanger remains pending for any coat or jacket I am currently wearing to school that day. The top shelf is dedicated to a minimalistic library of teacher curriculum resources and anthologies I own and/or frequent presently. A few other miscellaneous items remain tucked and stored away, along with simple backup items that are necessary for the school year.

The rest of the closet is not wasted. I utilized two plastic drawer organizers, one for additional office supply storage, student awards and prizes, pencil boxes, binder clips, classroom items, and the second for organizing frequented classroom copies. For example, there is a drawer dedicated to the classroom economy incentives, school-wide incentives, academic incentives (homework passes, standard home notes, etc.), a drawer dedicated to teacher-frequented office supplies, staples, push pins, pen packs, magnets, and clips, Ziploc or rubber bands. There is a remaining space of about a foot and a half between the two stacked towers and the shelf. For the remaining space, I leave that open for storing my lunch box and then for stacking other items when it is the end of the school year.

Shelves

The shelves are simple. They are additional resources you can utilize as a purposeful library or center that students will respect and gain a sense of academic pride and responsibility for, as well as feel comfortable accessing.

Students have access to shelves, not cabinets. Therefore, the shelves around the classroom are for student access. They should also be minimally maintained by students as well and contain purposeful items that will contribute to their academic environment. A library, academic resources, leveled readers in attractive bins, magazine stacks, games, and supplies if you are comfortable. Keep it simple, and remember the point of the classroom is to be a purposeful and immersive learning environment. Therefore, the mass of the items exposed within the classroom is for the benefit of student learning and/or their access. The few opportunities you have to store something behind a cabinet door, do so, and make it a mandatory rule that students do not go into the cabinets or any closed door or box without permission for that matter.

Do not feel confined or restricted to the idea that a bookshelf has to be utilized for books. Unless you are the reading and writing teacher – and maybe even if you are – you do not have to give away precious classroom space for "prop" hosting, meaning you are giving away a practical area within your classroom to items or things that are most often used or because that is the standard expectation. Throw those restrictive ideas and old laws out.

Instead, if you do not have purposeful books to store on your shelves, use them for something else. Bookshelves can make a great student center, a central location where students can access frequented items. An entire section is dedicated to what, who, and why every teacher should have one.

An organized assortment of leveled readers or circulators you change out with each unit or theme can be easily and attractively stored on shelves. Storing current manipulatives or lab and in-class experiment materials is another idea. A shelf countertop can also be used as a classroom learning location. I once saw a classroom where the teacher used the counter space along the windowsills as a computer station. It was a second-grade classroom, and she used stools as chairs for them to sit. It was a very practical idea. This also allowed for an additional free table to use for something else.

Shelf PIG: Keep it simple, purposeful, and immersive to the learning environment.

Cabinets

The rule I keep for cabinets is that cabinets are for storage, not students. Cabinets are great places for storing items you want to be kept out of sight and out of reach. When storing items and packing your cabinets, continue to keep cleanliness and organization at the front of your mind. If you are storing manipulatives, think bins and containers – easy to access, easy to transport, and easy to store and pack up. When you first pack your cabinets, two helpful ideas to keep in mind are access and long-term – what will you want to be kept up and out of the way but also access often and easily, and what can you store that you may need to periodically access, you may have a bulk amount of, and/or may keep or collect over a longer period of time?

In my current classroom, the cabinet and shelving system includes one half-wall of shelves, about twelve cubby holes, a half wall of cabinets, about three on the top layer and two on the bottom layer with the sink and a countertop between the two and one standard coat-size classroom closet.

The three cabinets above my sink each are each designated to a purpose of some kind. The farthest and hardest to reach house an oversupply of Ziplock bags, tissue boxes, and sanitizers. With the extra space, I store paint brushes and cups.

In the middle cabinet, which is located directly above the classroom sink, I store all items in regard to the sink, cleanliness, and houseware. On the top shelf, I keep overflow party supplies, napkins, paper plates, and cups and an estimated amount of tissue boxes for quick grabbing and replenishing around the room. On the second shelf of that cabinet, I store my round coffee mug, scrubbing brush, and dish soap. I keep the hand soap I actually use for my hands hidden and tucked away from little hands' overuse and the plastic flatware for easy access. I do not personally keep any Tupperware in the classroom, but I do keep a roll of plastic wrap and will use one of the spare paper plates or bowls if necessary.

The third cabinet is the most accessible cabinet, and that is where I store items I want to be kept out of sight but easy to grab. The bottom shelf is completely dedicated to storing the current open pack of copy paper I am using. The second side is where I keep the band-aids, spare breakfast supplies, and personal resource boxes. I currently only have two.

The final two cabinets are close to the bookshelves I have located along the classroom's wall of windows. This is where I store empty containers and hide the cleaning supplies. If you have not quite gotten a feel for my tone, I am definitely someone who admires a clean, sanitized, and minimized classroom. Inevitably, I have found myself with a few free spaces around the room. These spaces are great to have around for hiding or storing incoming supplies and materials gained throughout the school year.

Cabinet PIG: Out of sight and quick access storage. Maximize space.

PART TWO: CLASSROOM
WORK ZONE AND LOCATIONS

A teacher's workstation or teaching and presenting zone should be purposeful, accessible and easy to use and work from, similar to a cooktop. A sign of a sophisticated workstation is one that is frequented and transferable, meaning it does not have to be broken down or redesigned to suit the ever-changing needs of the classroom. It can operate across disciplines and hopefully activities. The location of working zone is important. Consider your audience and layout. Should your teacher work and presenting station be located in the front or the rear of the classroom, the middle of the classroom, or along the side? This one is a matter of preference, resources, and sometimes length of cords.

Over the years and with gratitude to working with an older grade, my workstations have now been simplified to a basket and carrying tray of sorts. In my basket, I usually have my tools, pens, highlighters, and any unusual or typical tool that we may need, things such as pencil and paper scholars are expected to have prepared. Notice the intentional language, "scholars are expected."

In my carrying tray, I usually have the presorted group folder, examples, rubrics, and/or other items I may find necessary for instruction and/or motivation, i.e., special supplies or incentives. That is all. I can

grab and go through my assortment at any time, and it is transferable to almost anywhere or anything we are doing. Using glue and scissors? Throw that in the basket. All sheets and collective items are in the tray.

◊ TEACHER DESK

This one can be a bit of a joke because of how rarely it can be used. You find it is that one location in the room you designate as your own and you wish you could actually get to use. Things just begin to gather on top of and in drawers. Eventually, you have no idea what those items are. The teacher's desk is an independent thing. Some may see use for one; others may not. If you rarely use it and could probably utilize another space such as your workstation or small group table for the same things you do at your desk and your school won't mind, get rid of the desk. You don't need it, and that space could be used for something else.

If you prefer a desk or do get a chance to use yours, keep it. The teacher desk is not mandatory. You are the commander of your classroom no matter where your bottom resides. The following section is a recommendation for teachers who do maintain a traditional teacher's desk.

No personal items except for your cell phone, mini emergency kit, and coin purse for the vending machine. If it goes missing, I know I have a thief, and it's a few dollars in change lost.

In the top drawer are my parent meeting and communications log, a basket for collecting miscellaneous teacher items such as pens, permanent markers, teacher scissors, and staple removers, and a container for collecting paper and binder clips. That's about it.

On a day-to-day basis, I add my phone and pencil pouch. My pencil pouch is one of the few teacher/school items that are allowed in my purse and can travel back and forth with me daily. The reason the pouch travels back and forth with me daily is that it is also the designated location for housing my badge when I am not wearing it, work flash or hard drive, and room keys when they are not around my neck or stored on the key hook above my desk.

The rest of my desk stores my lesson planner, workbag, and a Ziploc first aid kit for students or myself (a trick I learned from our school nurse to minimize trips).

You can make your own mini-emergency kit tailored to your needs. For emergency purposes, I also keep a small travel size make-up bag of personal items for and in the event of a personal emergency. A quick list includes the following: travel-sized toothbrush, toothpaste, floss, deodorant, and body spray. A miniature bottle of clear nail polish for stocking runs, one or two spare products for spontaneous pop-ups, if you know what I mean, but no medications. If found, those could be harmful to students. Any medications should travel back and forth within your purse that is kept locked up during instruction.

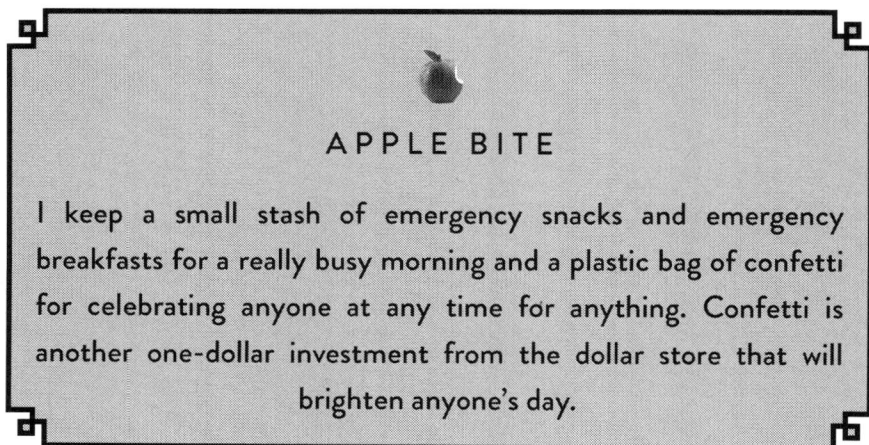

APPLE BITE

I keep a small stash of emergency snacks and emergency breakfasts for a really busy morning and a plastic bag of confetti for celebrating anyone at any time for anything. Confetti is another one-dollar investment from the dollar store that will brighten anyone's day.

◊ STUDENT DESK ARRANGEMENTS

There are so many different and various ideas for desks and how to arrange them; my best advice is to wait until you get into your classroom and make your first arrangement based on your student expectation and ability to move about the room. This portion of the layer you actually are just prepping. Do not finalize desks until you have completed layers two and three entirely. Otherwise, you will be scooting and unscooting.

I rarely choose student seats. The student chooses their own, and if I disagree with an arrangement, I will arrange accordingly. In holding true to a classroom design that fosters a learning environment, in addition to feeling like a home or designated place for learning, seating arrangements that favor groups, collaborations, and discussion are most preferred. At the older ages, I've found that they prefer to have their desks grouped and pushed together rather than in more open style patterns with vacancies in the middle. Those crafty desk layouts always seemed to find themselves pushed together into a team of lopsided contentment. I could push those desks apart until my hips ached, and they would still push or 'chat' themselves back together again.

◊ COMMAND CENTER: BOARDS

The command center is my favorite part of the classroom, and the boards are simple – think purposeful, engaging, and mandatory.

I love my boards. Each board is designated for something different. I even had to make a board for myself. There are two boards within my classroom designated to the district and schoolwide instructional responsibilities. In other words, I have a student work board and a current strategies and vocabulary board. The other boards are mine. Insert evil laugh.

My board is labeled "Teacher Center," including all things pertaining to me that need to be easily seen throughout the year. There's also a "Classroom News" board dedicated to all things class culture and explanations of our classroom behavior program and reward system, birthdays, schedules, a calendar with school and classroom updates and deadlines, lunch menus, and anything else the students or faculty may need in regards to student or classroom updates.

PIG of the boards: These are functional and used. No 'prop' boards!

Our biggest board complaints as teachers are use and updating. I agree it is a pain and time zapper to have to constantly update and maintain something you know is not being practically used. It looks good and practical, but outside of administration and the district, who else is looking at it? Certainly not the miniature people it is intended for. The students could care less, right?

I used to have that similar mentality until I decided that that was completely ridiculous, and if I was going to be required to update and use my boards, then so were my students. There was no time for impractical mandates. If I was mandated to use, I would find the practical way to mandate my students use it.

Those are the ideas here, students and use. Simply telling them or reading the information from the board to them each day is not a practical or productive use of my time and theirs. Instead, I decided to make it a little bit more engaging and a lot more of a priority.

The Main Board is the mandatory board. I dedicate the first ten minutes of each class to unpacking and reading the main board. During this time, I complete other tasks such as checking in and/or homework, quick imputing of information, or circulating. I have this time free because my students' entry routine requires them to read the board in order to know what to do. They know that they have a ten-minute timer to unpack, gather their materials, copy their homework down, and at least be getting started or have started their entry warmup or engagement.

Everything they need to know and how to do it is located somewhere on that main board. In addition to the objectives, which I do not expect them to read, are locations for the homework, materials for the day, a big idea or a concept focus of the week we will be referencing or adding to, an agenda briefly highlighting the day, a daily morning message, the date, and a weekly quote. The projector will project anything on a separate screen if the entry assignment requires projecting.

I don't tell the students anything. They very quickly begin to learn to rely on the boards and not myself or their peers to tell what to do or how to get started. The timer element gives them an urgency to start. I don't require a ten-minute finish because that would produce works of no real value, and the real intention of these first ten minutes is to get the students to read and comprehend the board. Once the timer has gone off, I greet my students and summarize the homework and key ideas form the daily message. This is the routine each and every single day. It never changes. This not only makes the reading of the board a mandatory routine; it also gives me guaranteed instructional time to review the objectives and explain the homework to students. Before I started this routine, I found myself sometimes forgetting to state the objective and scrambling to go over and pass out the homework. With the ten-minute board opening routine, the students and I are both given a window to go over these things before every lesson.

When considering the setup and design of your board, keep it simple, engaging, intentional, and mandatory. I discussed the intentions and reasons for why reading the board is mandatory. Here are the reasons for the quote for maintaining an engaging board. It keeps it fun! Inspiration or thought-provoking quotes get dynamic conversations started and students thinking constructive or creatively. The key, like anything, is you have to enforce the idea. Have fun with it. I usually begin the year with an intentionally selected quote each week for the first couple of months. Every Monday, a student volunteer reads the quote and selects peers to interpret. As time goes on and the class becomes custom to the routine, the responsibility is transferred to the students, and students are required to select, donate, or develop inspirational or motivational quotes to be chosen each week. That's when things really start to get fun.

The students look forward to sharing their quotes and perspective each week. I didn't come up with the idea entirely on my own. I also enjoyed the idea of beginning the week with a quote, but I didn't start reading it aloud each week or getting students involved routinely until years later. That began with a book. It began with a children's book of precepts for each day of the year I bought at the school's book fair. I had been introduced to the intial book a few years prior during one

71

of my summer school experiences and really liked the way the author incorporated the concept of empathy into their novel.

I loved R. J. Palacio's story *Wonder* when I first read it and assumed the follow-up book of precepts would be just as good. That year, I had the students read the precept of the day each morning. At first, they weren't into it but didn't protest doing it each morning. Before I knew it, they took over the idea and started to create their own and then asked to have theirs posted on the board for the weekly quote. Of course, I said yes, and after that, it became the thing to see what the quote would be and who was going to get theirs posted. To keep it spontaneous and also utilize my opportunities for exposure, the quotes weren't the student's every week. Some weeks, I was strategic in connecting the quote to our units or objectives; other times they were completely random and credited to other individuals of the world. Board quoting is also a phenomenal tool for changing classroom dynamics and influencing class culture.

Each day the date, daily message, homework, and student materials are updated. Objectives are updated according to lessons, whether that be daily or several times a week. The daily message is the running record and reiteration of objective and lesson focus. This is where the record of what happened in the prior lesson, what's happening in today's lesson and what the plan will be to do with the information next. Key vocabulary for the lesson or day, any specialty, information, and what is being assessed or due at the end of the lesson. The daily message is a key component to my board and for my students. If you adopt these methods, try to keep it interesting and not too wordy. A similar format for each time helps, but don't use a sentence-starter fill-in-the-blank style. They will learn to skim that. Add a joke or secret message in there from time to time. One of my favorites is about three lines in, I'll add in, "If you are reading this, place a pencil on your ear or in your hair. Keep it a secret between me, you and the readers of this message only." Its engaging, simple, and fun. It encourages them to check the message each day even if they aren't reading, and the students love to feel like they are in on a secret.

LAYER THREE: FINALIZING WORK ZONES, FURNITURE, AND TECHNOLOGY

FURNITURE ARRANGEMENTS

When completing this part of your classroom, the location and arrangement of your furniture should be thoughtful and final for the most part. Never fear changing things up or rearranging your classroom at any time throughout the year. I have a colleague that does this at any given time. One random day, she will have her entire classroom redesigned. She claims it's her Sagittarius trait. I learned too every so often it's necessary to switch things up. I love it. The students say "wow" the first day and acclimate by the next. When the end of the week comes, the students have completely adapted to the new system and let go of the old.

ZONING

When establishing locations, think about the purpose for each area — what items would make that both possible and practical? How do I create

or establish this space where access and cleanup are both easy to achieve? Then manipulate and arrange your furniture to achieve these ideas.

As you read through the following components, keep in mind that these are general suggestions, and ultimately, you must decide, adapt, add, and change to suit your teaching style and the needs of your classroom. This is your classroom kitchen!

When you have arrived at the third layer of classroom unpacking, your classroom should have a pretty solid skeleton of what your functioning classroom will look like. In this layer, it is now time to finalize your furniture arrangements. The ideas for function and location should have already been established for all of your workstations, centers, and zones. Push items up against the wall if you haven't already, roll out your rug, and plug in your technology.

This layer is also a great time to begin assigning duties and tasks if you have the opportunity for help. You have unpacked all the necessary items that require stern thought; all of your locations are assigned and the skeletons upright, making for this layer of the cake perfect for assistance.

In this layer, it is also important to consider your zones – your zones for working, where your small groups will meet, your class meetings held, etc. I have provided a few classroom zones as ideas. You can organize and have each location prepared so that your assistant's only task is shelf stocking or plugging up the technology, putting up the headers to a board that will later host student work, etc. Whatever you choose, however you choose, it is in this layer; if opportunity allows, you will not only benefit the most greatly in this layer but also be the most prepared to receive and delegate tasks.

STUDENT ZONES

The carpet is an excellent location for hosting class meetings and discussions. If you do not have or prefer carpets, consider designing one location in the room where students could turn their chairs and face the opposite direction to symbolize and physically represent when class meetings are being held.

Consider a student center location for students to access common and frequented materials. Establish the procedures for access and cleanup and decide if you can allow students to have autonomy and independence when it comes to the student center. It will save you time and effort in addressing hands that are only asking for pencils and supplies.

If you have cubbies or other odd areas within your classroom, these areas can be used as academic areas for students to retreat too in groups or independently to complete assignments. You can even make these areas reward ideas. Scholars can strive to earn 'academic zone' passes or 'buddy passes' to work in these areas with peers.

REGARDS FOR LAYING WIRES, CORDS AND PLACING TECHNOLOGY

You should now also feel comfortable setting up and plugging in all of your technology. Each school and district will have its own guidelines and policies for school equipment. My personal rule of thumb for professional equipment is to move with the idea, "You break it; you are responsible for the replacement of it," and to try and treat each item better than my own, no matter how old, how funky and temperamental it may be. I intend to respect each piece and protect each piece as thoughtfully as I can. The following are not necessarily a list of rules, rather an acquisition of tips for all classroom furniture and materials and specifically for technology.

Tech Tips:

1. Dust, Mites, Temperature, and Water

   • Try to never place technology near liquid stations or places with very quick temperature changes or extreme temperatures. Areas within your classroom that you know are highly trafficked by insects, spiders, or rodents, you may want to reconsider designating them as home to anything honestly but especially technology because of all the little crevices and wires.

   • The term "mites" is not necessarily specific or particular to actual living mites. The term mite is more specific to things, tiny beads of glue balls, sticky surfaces, eraser dust, pencil shavings, and pencil lead bits, just the general collection of classroom particles that tend to matriculate into existence.

2. Hide and Tuck Wires

   • Another obvious one, and for that reason, I will skip the why and share tips on the how.

   • Think minimal. The least amount of cords, the better. If that means moving things closer and rearranging, try that as an option. Speaking with your building supervisor or making a request to your main office for a cord strip to protect against accidental incidents is also a healthy alternative.

3. Designate Locations and Operations

- Students should be able to utilize the resources and have independent access to certain things within the classroom. Create a routine or procedure for how to use and put up all equipment when not in use.

- If you have listening centers or computer centers, post a simple chart of procedures for proper use in that location. This will save time in constantly repeating your expectation. You can reinforce the anchor chart.

- Give all computer mice, keyboards, and remotes a designation and procedure for use and clean up. This also makes it easy to locate remotes in the event of a substitute or staff member need to use the remote and I am not in the room.

LAYER FOUR: WALLS

Walls are for motivational posters if and only if they motivate and/or make you chuckle too. Otherwise, walls are for anchor charts, resource charts, display of student products or expectations, schedules, and information. Keep it simple. You do not have to fill every inch of the wall with items you bought from the store or ordered online, and if you do, that is your choice, but what are they for? Remember the classroom is an extension of your instruction and can also be used as a functional learning tool.

Dedicate wall space to ideas you want students to absorb, things that are unique to your classroom culture (I have a classroom signals board for new students and visitors), and things that reinforce your

classroom or school culture. Skip over the catchy slogans and cartoon scenes and opt for posters that are biographical or actually replicas of primary sources and quotes from famous persons or students that inspire or relate to your current theme. Having a visually stimulating and attractive classroom is so much more powerful when these posters are intentionally placed and selected. I suggest you substitute cute for content, but do not sink the room in anchor and instructional charts or over-do it with meaningless space occupiers.

When putting up wall décor, try to complete this step in one session. Dedicate a sufficient amount of time, and gather all your necessary materials – hot glue gun, command strips, tape, staples, push pins, scissors, etc., and keep them in a basket for easy moving around the room. Then do a temporary layout of the arrangement for each poster or wall decoration in each location. Next, take a small bit of tape, roll it around your finger so that it becomes double-sided, and temporarily stick each poster on the wall before you finalize the design. When you are certain, take a pencil and lightly pencil mark each spot; then gather your material basket and start finalizing.

It is my recommendation to leave this step for almost last because one slight push of a table and an entire arrangement of wall mounts becomes off-centered. Trust me; I have put up and taken down a set of wall posters so many times that I was convinced that an entire school year with an off-centered Teacher Center board and downward-sloping inspirational quote would be completely fine and found that to be completely true.

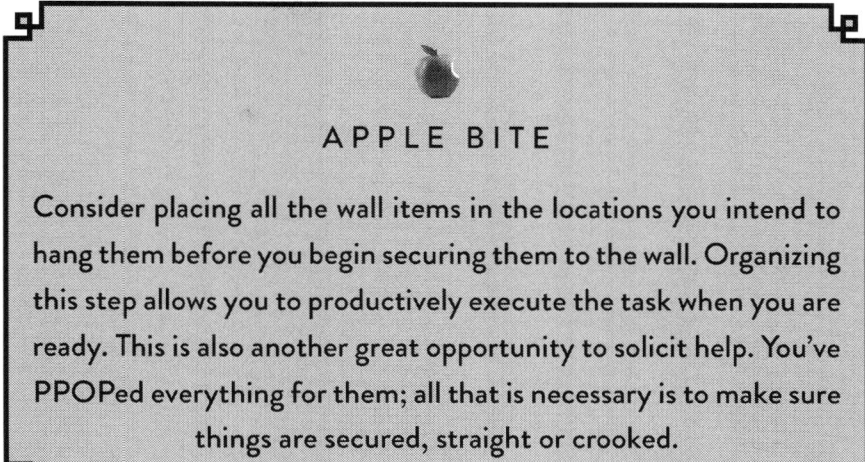

APPLE BITE

Consider placing all the wall items in the locations you intend to hang them before you begin securing them to the wall. Organizing this step allows you to productively execute the task when you are ready. This is also another great opportunity to solicit help. You've PPOPed everything for them; all that is necessary is to make sure things are secured, straight or crooked.

LAYER FIVE: CLASSROOM DESIGN, DÉCOR, ROUTINES AND LABELS

Finally, Layer Five – this is the layer you are actually thinking and dreaming about. We all envision the décor, design, and done phase. This is the phase we hope the whole process could be, adding our special touches, and *voila!* a complete classroom. Well, now you have arrived and have learned the process of getting there in three days. Get your glue gun and shopping bags; here comes the fun!

CLASSROOM THEMES AND DECOR

Classroom decor is such a simple effort that really can make all the difference in a classroom. It is the little extra effort that shows you care and that you're invested beyond the career. You're there because you want to be there, because you love it, and décor does not make or break those ideas. However, the decor is important and can really make

a room if you decide to go that route. Remember. Classroom Kitchen – everyone's design is their own.

Décor has the ability to read across a room and down a hallway without ever saying a word. It can speak for you, communicating your style, your expectations, and where you spent your efforts of time. The décor factor of the classroom is left to your discretion. Personally, I would go with a "less is more" policy – an area or two that has an interchanging monthly scene or trinket is a satisfyingly simple way to decorate and efficiently update.

The design and routines of your classroom were thought out during your second assessment in layer one, and you have been implementing these ideas along the way of unpacking. When it comes to this layer, designing your classroom routine is a matter of placing labels, baskets, and bins and double-checking the efficiency and fluidity of the design. Does it make sense to have the students travel across the room to turn things in or have it closer to the entry and exit? Does the furniture design allow for safe and quick maneuvering about the classroom? Do you want to add a plant in the windowsill, by the sink, or not at all?

This is also where you can add your touches and themed ideas. This layer is dedicated to allowing you the time to decorate and design your classroom kitchen the way you desire, knowing the rest of the work is complete. After you complete this final layer, your classroom unpacking process has been sophisticatedly simplified, PPOPed and ready for student entry. You can spend the rest of your week participating in staff meetings without the pressures of your classroom hanging over your shoulder and the rest of your days planning and lesson building for the first weeks of school.

END OF THE YEAR PACK UP

When the end of the year comes, repeat this process following layer one, assessment two, and intentionally plot out the most productive way to pack up your classroom layout for seamless and productive unpacking next school year. Next, move through packing up layers three and four, take down walls, and begin to back up zones. Then complete layers two and five together. The final step is to complete layer one assessment one and do that final clean before summer. I recommend beginning the pack-up process gradually and then all at once. Move through layers two and three gradually, and when you feel it is best, complete final two and a half layers all at once and within a three-day window. Don't forget to PIG and PPOP before you begin!

CHAPTER 5

CHAPTER 5

"PIG, PPOP, Instruct!"
– How to Effectively PPOP in Instructional Planning

" What does the sophisticated teacher look like? Well planned, well managed, well balanced. Well dressed, not stressed, punctual, God-serving, and God-fearing. All they preach in common core are standards, and I want to be anything but standard or common. I want to hold myself accountable to the standard of teaching I decree, the one I know I can uphold with consistency and pride.

"Next year will be a completely different year. The same goes for the remainder of this year.

Things to improve upon...

1. Pacing. I noticed if no one is on top of me as far as deadlines, neither am I. Hold myself accountable.

2. Punctuality. Arrive to work early. Meetings and deadlines promptly.

3. PPOP Teacher. Planned Organized and Prepared. Well managed includes being well planned. I've built the systems; it's all a matter of obedience and follow-through. The act of consistently doing.

4. Procrastination. There is no longer such a thing. As soon as possible, it's in my hands to respond or complete. No back orders.

5. No homework. I hate homework and weekend work. During the week and my work hours are for work. Get it done.

6. Goals. Set them and respect them. Set them often. Respect them always.

7. Purpose. God has placed me here to work for a reason and for purpose. Above all else maintain Faith, sophistication, and grace."

This was sent from my iPhone circa late 2015 during the 2015-2016 school year. I was sick of spending my nights, weekends, and everything else consumed with planning, thinking about it or avoiding it. I wrote this note to myself as a set of principles and foundations for instruction, and that concludes the prerequisite portion. Now, you may proceed into your lessons.

LESSON PLANNING MATRIX

Planning – what a monster of a word. Eight very important strategically placed letters forming one of the most essential components of teaching. It took me ages to get myself into a place and flow where I am not spending hours upon hours attempting to plan and then leaving the session with an incomplete one. There are few things more frustrating and overwhelming than attempting to plan, believing you have done it, committing the time in planning, and then having to go home just to do the same thing. Oh, planning can suck. Even worse is the gracious amount of people willing to help you plan while, in fact, they are hardly helping at all.

In this chapter, we will discuss a few strategies and tips for planning, as well as how to effectively, efficiently, and exceptionally execute planning with sophistication and simplicity. I have tried a few things – more than a few. And while trial and error can be frustrating at times, I have had enough trials to say I've tested it, it worked for me, and I have learned enough to share and help another. Caring is sharing, after all.

LESSON PLANNING BASICS

There are so many layers and components to planning, even before you get to the lesson planning, as well as steps after. That is one of the first things I want you to know. Planning is done in layers, steps, phases (coin your key term), but the point is it is not done in one day. It absolutely can be – I have the late nights and stress badges to prove it. Sometimes it has to be, but it does not have to be all the time. It is better to come prepared with a refreshed mind and strategically break planning apart. Breaking the process of planning into phases also allows room for designating certain parts of the process to other people if you are planning collaboratively.

The next thing is you are going to have to read everything at least twice: the curriculum, the standards, the actual lesson you create, the resources, etc. You need to look over and thoroughly read at least twice. Curriculum reading is not juicy or poetic. It tends to be very formal, overly exaggerated, or thoroughly under-detailed and direct. "You say… Students respond… Tell the students… Guide, turn, then say…" Does any of this sound familiar?

Expect a lot of reading to be involved, and don't hate it. Come prepared to do some very plain and authoritative reading, bring your snack,

your beverage treats, and your pencil pouch of office-supply goodness. Enjoy the reading and curriculum-reviewing portion of planning. It is very important that you have a thorough understanding of the material prior to teaching it. It is equally important that you are aware of your standards and objective goals and how you are expressing and referring back to them throughout the lesson. So you cannot skip or skim this part. Enjoy it. Highlight and color-code strategically. Annotate and keep alongside a notebook or sticky pad to pull out your information to build upon and to put the questions you develop for yourself as you are learning. Try to maintain the same journal for planning so you can reference it later and respond to questions you may have written down. Consider this first phase your student and study time. This is your time as a student to be introduced to new material and plan out the *whats* and *hows* of it all.

This phase is also the only phase of planning I will allow in my home. I actually prefer it. I can be snuggled up, more relaxed, and take my time with a lot fewer interruptions. This may even be the pre-phase of planning. How can you even begin planning if you don't have your direction or know your why? The remaining phases should be done at school.

The final thing I want you to know before planning is that proper planning is an investment. This investment requires time, mental energy, and commitment to the task. Think of it as an investment, a major investment that if you make the choice now to invest fully into will pay off greatly for you later. It's a money upfront kind of deal. Don't put in half now and skirt the rest of onto a payment plan over time. Do it now. Put all the money down now and walk away with a lucrative return.

With that being said, I like to plan in units. My daily plans are completed and built from/within the unit plan. The unit plan is complete and organized in a format that is readable and fluid for – this one is superiorly important – *me*. Does that mean I often have to take apart work that is already – rather claims to have already been – done for me? Yes. Yes, it does. I do it anyway. I do it anyway because if I do it the right way for me, once, I'll never have to do it again. Tweaks and updates understood. I don't reinvent the wheel. I customize it, add rims and a spoiler. My wheels are spinning.

Alrighty, well that's planning basics, prerequisites one, two, and three. Now we can begin from the bottom up. Have you heard of the term backwards planning? You should become familiar with not only the term but also the method. It is to plan backward, with the end in mind first. Instead of planning from the first lesson objective to the assessment of your lessons or unit, identify what your assessment is and what the incremental evaluations and standards are that you will be assessing along the way first. Next, pull out your vocabulary, tools, strategies, and resources that are provided. Then, take a look at all of that in relation to what is being assessed, develop your objectives, and then finally begin the process of developing lesson plans and lesson sequencing.

Plan with the mindset of "I am planning a unit. It comprises of several lessons relating to the same topic covering a range of relatable standards across various degrees of rigor." Rarely plan with the mindset of one single lesson. That comes up at a later phase after you have

established where you are going and what you will expect from getting there. Then we can work on the plan to get there.

When you're backwardly planning your units, it will greatly benefit you to have a template where you record all the necessary information you will need. It is important that you are collecting the information in a fluid and formal manner that you will be able to read and access year after year for edits and use. Remember, planning is an investment. You will not want to have to commit such immense amounts of time each day or even each week if you really make a huge initial investment for your lesson planning. Realistically, as the year progresses, you may find it harder and harder to commit such thorough amounts of time into planning each day. Your instruction, your students, and your practice will suffer because of it. Trust me. Make the investment upfront, make it big, and make it once!

Let's begin PPOP planning!

PPOP PLANNING PHASES

Prepared, Planned, Organized, and Productive – PPOP. It's an acronym and framework for planning I have used since I made the choice to revamp my practice. With modifications, I have learned that those simple words in that simple order can be applied to almost anything, and the outcomes are almost always the same – success.

I have planned many ways within my time – the long, time-consuming and excruciating ways mostly. Proper planning, I have found, is its own phase and step in itself. You actually have to be prepared for planning before you can even begin planning. Otherwise, you will find yourself with constant starts and stops and very little footwork, eventually ending up exhausted, or worse, you will become the quick grab-and-compile planner.

If your lessons include very little rigor and consist primarily of practice and busywork, the facts are you are just not investing enough time into your lesson plan development process. You are not an ineffective teacher; your lesson planning just needs some improving. Quick lessons may have great skeletons. You may even have skin over the bones, but the dressing, the accessory, the style, the distinguishing and echelon qualities would have been remiss. Commit today to stop quick-grabbing your lessons and wondering why you're exhausted or students are not making consistent grains. The fact is you are really all over the place and shooting in the air hoping something sticks. Tell the truth; the ole 'some learning is better than none' or 'it's practice' excuses are only excusing the lack of time you managed and invested into planning. If your target is the ground, you will land success almost every time with little effort. If you are actually aiming for a target, focus your aim, and elevate your practice.

We all fluctuate to some degree between the two realms — the extremes of committing my complete self and all I have into developing the best lessons the classroom has ever seen and I am just getting this done, period. It is a reality, and it can especially be a reality if you are not properly allocating time and energy into the process of planning lessons. Your lessons can and will be wonderfully engaging and attractive, but that does not make it great. Always remember when planning it is about the objective, instructing and fostering the learn-

ing of what is being evaluated to your students. How you get there is where you can have fun, but the purpose is the main intent.

Achieving that purpose, with data to back it up, defines a great lesson. So, in short, always remain grounded in your top three: the objective, the pathway to learning, and how am I assessing or evaluating the achievement of the objective? Evaluating and assessing students' grasp of concept and depth of knowledge along the way are the best ways to monitor, target, and achieve student growth. So, plan accordingly.

Because unpacking and planning an entire unit is such a cumbersome job, I break the task apart into, you guessed it, phases. My goal is always to have my complete PPOP preparations for the next week done in three days.

PHASE ONE: "P IS FOR PREPARED!" PREPARING TO PLAN

Prepare to Plan references exactly what the three terms describe: to have taken the steps necessary to effectively prepare and develop a well-designed plan for instruction and implementation. When you are preparing to plan, obviously it is important to have the information and materials you will need alongside you, but do you know what those materials are?

LOCATE: DATA, STANDARDS, AND CURRICULUM MATERIALS

The first item on the list for the preparation phase of PPOP is the student pretest data. This is one of the most beneficial pieces of information you will need when it comes to planning your student baseline. You need to know where they are concept-wise in order to establish where you're going and the route to get there.

Data, data, data. I hated those four letters when I first began teaching. I have since learned to love them. With all things in life, you have to know how and why to use it. Those two points alone have inspired hundreds of books on the topic. If there were any identifiable trends or significantly low pockets and high scores, include those as your planning priorities when lesson developing. The high pocket scores should not be dismissed and checked off with the idea that the students have the standard mastered and completely understood. Data is black and white in concrete terms, but it is abstractly gathered. Therefore, mark it as a great tool but not the end all be all.

High pocket scores can be used for lesson extension ideas expanding on the rigor and enrichment opportunities since you may not need to spend much time introducing this concept. You may be able to focus on diving deeper into the standard, possibly incorporating independent study opportunities for students as a rotation. Be sure to still periodically assess and incorporate the standard as you teach through the unit. It would be problematic if the students came to the end and suddenly forgot how or lost the information.

Here's a favorite elementary school song sung by students: "But you never taught us that." As I point to worksheets, posters, and board objectives with said information located in plain view. It's not necessarily their fault, of course; you taught it or exposed them to it. They may have enjoyed the lesson, had a blast, earned an A on the assignment,

and all, but if you never circle back and bring it back up, it was a one-and-done lesson.

Students collectively do not own that information. They have it. They can dig for it probably or are doing it naturally, but sometimes if it's never mentioned again, they believe they've never heard its name. Learning is actually not like riding a bike. It is more like walking. You really have to intentionally keep putting one foot in front of the other, have a fall down, intentionally get back up, and yep, one foot in front of the other again. "Repeat!" However, if you keep them walking, eventually, they'll begin to run, and you start arriving at your instructional destinations a lot faster. You should still circle back every now and again, but your students may begin to refer back and recall past information and lessons gained on their own once the habit and routine are engrained.

Keep it very simple and always begin your units with an assessment aligned with the standards and objectives you will be teaching for the time. One that favors the format students will face in formal testing will always be beneficial. Always close units with an assessment parallel evaluating the same standards. Be sure you are aware of which questions are aligned to which standard and require what skills so that you can accurately identify and utilize the pre- and post-data for the next steps in instruction. Take the same idea and apply it, formatively assessing along the way, strategically targeting and setting growth targets along the way before the final assessment.

You will also be locating your curriculum, your state standards, the workbook, and student resource materials you will be using. The first step in planning is preparing for it. Have all the necessary tools and materials for planning and all the necessary tools and materials and designations for what to do after planning has been completed. My first step in planning after reading is always completing my matrix templates, then lesson or instructional plan development, and gathering materials.

UNPACKING

The next tool in preparation is to unpack. This would be where you use whatever you are using to collect and organize your information while unpacking your curricula. Some school districts offer templates for unpacking; some districts unpack the standards for you already; some don't at all. Either way, if you're in need, I've got this one covered.

I have a Unit Opener Matrix as well as several other correlating matrixes that I developed for planning. I have benefited a great deal when using this consistently. It is also translatable, but remember the most important thing is that you are using a format and design that is functional and readable for… *you*!

After my first curriculum read, I go back in and start pulling the instructional information I will need for teaching. Typically, I am only inputting into the unit opener once every month and a half or so. The unit opener unpacks the whole unit; from there, I begin unpacking and compiling the instructional information I will need for teaching into my unit lesson plan template. There is also where the actual lesson developing and lesson plans will be built during the next PPOP phase, *planning*. It takes a commitment to complete the job, but once it is done, the goal is that it is done completely. It is an investment of time for sure, but it pays off lucratively. And as mentioned, when done consistently, your speed will increase in the following years; so long as the standards have not changed, you can pull and reference past lessons. The only thing you would need to do is review and update your lessons with any new strategies or ideas you've gained.

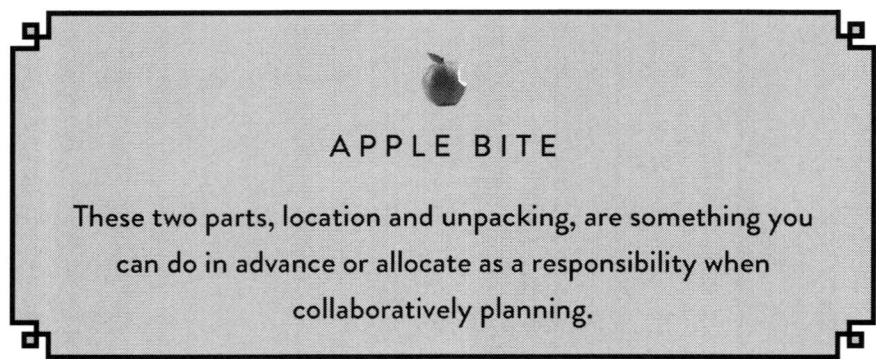

APPLE BITE

These two parts, location and unpacking, are something you can do in advance or allocate as a responsibility when collaboratively planning.

PHASE TWO: "P IS FOR PLANNED!" LESSON PLANNING, STRUCTURE, AND CYCLES

The second part of PPOP is planning. Within this phase, lesson building and development take place. I try to complete these two steps within two days. Anything that needs to be modified, adapted, or created is completed during this phase as well, usually the second day. Remember to proofread any self-made resources. Either way, everyone makes mistakes, and you will inevitably make one as well. Try your best to not only proofread for mistakes, but also check for fluency, alignment, and opportunities to incorporate vocabulary or other skills. Don't over-complicate an assignment, but if you can pump it up and still serve the objective, why not go for it?

Another major part of planning includes the additional investment of time and resources you will either be creating, printing, locating, or some combination of all three. The resources and materials for the lesson are almost equally as important as the lesson. Don't forget them, don't shortchange them, and don't get exhausted because of them. Plan for that component accordingly.

LESSON PLAN BUILDING
AND STRUCTURE

This is another area that can be very specific to your school or district. Everyone does it differently, but there are some consistencies across most schools. Your lesson plans usually have a format. This format can be anything from a three-part process to a complex twelve steps, and if your school district policy is to abide by all twelve or all three steps, do so with integrity.

Thankfully, the format does not matter so much as the purpose and process for evaluating do. Here are my recommended basic fundamentals of any lesson plan. You should certainly elaborate, but please never ever skip these four components. The components are:

1. a beginning that includes vocabulary or academic terms and clearly defined objectives for learning
2. a middle that includes immersion and expansion for students to process and apply while exploring and elaborating on the objective
3. an end that evaluates students' overall achievement of the objective or standard
4. some sort of formal or informal assessment along with each step of the process.

LESSON CYCLES

Lesson cycles are a term I use to describe the ideal routine in which to implement lessons. I mentioned that I prefer to teach in a unit. If and when I can, I try to optimize my lesson planning and instructional time by minimizing the number of lessons I teach and instead focus on maximizing the impact and potential outcomes from the lessons. I try to plan in three lessons taught over the course of five to seven ses-

sions max, preferably five. The additional lessons can be described as reteaching, interventions, or elaboration lessons. I focus my attention on a three-phase process and then repeat the cycle as needed, preferably through the next set of unit objectives.

The phases of the four-day lesson cycles are a unit introductory lesson, the opening lesson, the check-in and expansion lesson, and the evaluation lesson, assessing goal marks along the way. Each transition is dependent on the outcomes of the step before. Open the lesson. Assess against the established goal. Based on level of success, move into check-in and expansion. Assess students' progress thus far and ability to apply the concept. Based on level of success, move into the next lesson, an evaluating lesson.

The opening lesson is your very first lesson and begins after the unit introduction lesson, which would include instructional components such as giving the pre-assessment and introducing the vocabulary, establishing and dissecting the standards and objectives for the unit as a class, developing a rubric, and having students predict or develop their 'pre' ideas about the unit. An example of an 'opening lesson' would be the first official assessment aligned lesson of the unit and could also include expanding or applying the vocabulary.

A 'check-in and expansion' lesson example should include an evaluation of some sort marking student progress. Use the data from the progress evaluation to inform the next steps. This lesson should focus on the practice and application of the skills from the opening lesson and could include elaborating or expanding upon topics. It is a wise idea to prepare those elements of them anyway for lesson flexibility and fluidity while teaching. It is much easier to be able to just change directions during a lesson and jump into something than have to create it along the way. An example of an evaluation lesson should include an assessment tool that will produce measurable data and is aligned with the pre-assessment. Don't fret because it will align because you already took the time to locate and prepare this during the prepare to plan phase previously. Remember, make the investment all at once!

PHASE THREE: "O IS FOR ORGANIZED!" ORGANIZATION, OVERVIEWING, AND OPTIMIZING

After my lessons have been developed, the next phase of planning is organizing all the information, materials, resources, and gathered hard work. There is no bigger let-down than taking the time and effort to develop your lesson plans and then forgetting to properly prepare for them and have the instructional outcomes be disorganized and lackluster. Don't even put yourself in the pot.

The organization phase is one of the most important parts (well, they are all important parts), but it is the most important part of productivity. This phase involves establishing your print list of all the copies you will need and how they will need to be copied, organizing your rotations and students for small group instruction, the order and time frames for implementing each lesson (for example, reading math may be every day, but science is three times a week at teacher discretion). I call the organization of the weekly schedule the weekly script. The instructional framework primarily stays the sometimes even the fundamental wordings of the words. This is usually because it is the school

district that assigns the instructional frameworks and time allotments. Any other resources that need to be gathered that are not created or printed such as manipulatives, workbooks, and books – those are gathered and organized during this phase too. Labels are some of your best resources for this phase. Overview and optimization refer to looking over your lesson plans, proof reading, and then checking to ensure you have optimized every opportunity to maximize your instructional impact and growth targets.

APPLE BITE

This phase can also be allocated and designated if collaborative planning with a team.

PHASE FOUR: "THIS P IS FOR PRODUCTIVITY!" PRODUCTIVE EXECUTION

This is my favorite part of PPOPing – the execution. The send to the printer, place in their daily folders or bins and done part! This is the part of PPOPing where I usually bask in having completed my lesson planning for the coming week, maybe even a rough skeleton for the next couple of weeks. Depending on how much content and standards are covered in a unit, you may be able to PPOP for a whole unit and have your lessons basically planned for the quarter. I haven't met this glory often, but when I commit to doing, the reward is so great. I end up with so much additional free time I barely know what to do with myself. I often end up in a conversation chatting away thinking I have time to kill. Thankfully, I do, but that time was made free to accomplish other things. But, a good side chit-chat with a colleague every now and again is good for the soul.

In the productivity phase, you should be submitting or copying the items of your print list and then sorting them into the folders or assigned locations you have for each day's lesson plan and accompanying work and resources. In this phase, the resources you need for your lessons should have already been designated, sorted, and labeled during the organization phase. While it is best to follow the PPOP order, you are not obligated. I also stress and encourage you to adapt to and for you! I tend to stick to the PPOP order, but I overlap some phases. For the sake of time and productivity, some things like printing can take place while other things are, like preparing my next unit matrix or sorting materials; to be productive.

APPLE BITE

Use a timer. Designate a timeframe for completing each phase like forty-five minutes and commit to effectively completing as much as you can with fidelity within the time frame. You may miss the mark in the beginning, but eventually, you will train yourself to complete each step of the phase, degree depending, within whatever time frame you set for yourself.

MODEL PPOP: WEEKLY SCHEDULE: MONDAY THROUGH FRIDAY

PHASE ONE: PREPARED TO PLAN AND PLANNING

Matrix Mondays and Tuesday PPOP Preparations

I have realized that I actually never want to jump right into lesson planning on Mondays. The sheer thought of it makes my eyes want to dart up at the clock and count the minutes before I can leave and run out the door to the sanctity of my home, only to be slowed down by the weight of a workbag filled with the work I intended to skip out on planning. But at last, reality strikes. Of course, it must be planned. And that sanctity of the home, so free and comforting, is now a reality of completing work-at-home in comfortable pajamas.

I've learned to find ways to enjoy planning at home, so much as you learn to enjoy swallowing liquid medicine as a child. We make that bitter, inevitable "I hate this, but I know I have to do it because it's what's good for me" face. Oh, how I hated moments such as that, but we do them, we get over them, and we are better and thankful for it in the end.

Except I decided I couldn't live my life, continue to live my life, making that face. I hate homework. I also can be completely over-whelmed by the processes of planning. I stopped to take a look at why. I was constantly trying to build Rome in a day and panicking about the onset of Greece. In short, I was out of order and doing way too much. I have learned to find an efficient way of managing the planning process for me. Mondays and Tuesdays, I tackle my first Ps, preparing to plan and actual lesson plan developing. Because Monday I prefer to spend most of my workable energy interacting with students and setting the tone for my work week, I usually do not spend much mental energy lesson planning. I tackle more mindless tasks such as completing my planning matrixes, looking over the curriculum and plotting my lesson plans. Matrix Monday is the catchphrase.

Mondays are where I prepare all the necessary materials for planning and strategically plotting. Tuesday is actual lesson planning day stretching into Wednesday. While I lesson plan, I also make it a point to refer back to my templates and complete the resources and materials print list sections. This makes my Wednesday organization much more fluid. I can simply add items to a print folder while planning. When it's time, in the productive phase I can check off as I print and sort directly into locations, etc. Any leftover planning I try to complete during my Wednesday morning planning period.

PHASE TWO: ORGANIZATION

Wednesday Organizing, Optimizing, Overviewing and Weekly Scripting aka 'WOOOW'

Wednesday is for *O, organization,* after planning is complete.

On Wednesday, I check over my lesson plans and then begin the process drafting or plotting my weekly script for when each lesson will be taught. Finalize what will be printed and the print counts, creating or prepping any resources, pulling resources, developing anchor charts, vocabulary cards, any and all things such as that are done on Wednesdays. I gather my print list, my weekly print list bundles, lesson plans,

matrixes, everything. It is lovely when the first P, preparation, is done by Tuesday because I can usually get most of this done during my morning planning period. This leaves my actual planning period for the second P, planning or to begin grading. Grading has got to be done at some point. The more on top of and consistent you stay with your grades, the better idea you have about how your students are doing.

While developing any lesson resources, I organize and label them according to the sequence of use, meaning the materials and lesson plans for the first lesson are all bundled and organized in an accessible manner and labeled for the first day. The same for the second, third, and so on until the next actual lesson. As well as considering and allocating which assignments will be graded. This is where grades-to-be are identified and assigned for each lesson plan. Resources that will be reused in future lessons are labeled as such so that they are not packed away at the end of the lesson, but instead at the end of the unit. This makes for an organized as well as productive flow in planning. When I am really on it, I can complete most of this while copies are printing. By the time I leave the copy room, I may have complete weeks planned, organized, and prepared for teaching. I just have to review the lesson plan or lesson skit and begin. It is absolutely lovely.

PHASE THREE: PRODUCTIVELY PREPARED TO EXECUTE

Thursday Tackle: Productively Prepare and Friday Executions: Productively Execute for the Coming Week

The final phase is P, productively prepare. Having taken the time to be prepared productively, these are the days I take to actually map and physically sort out my instruction for the week. For example, a math lesson may be broken apart across two days before the next one begins. Schedule the remaining subject disciplines and their lesson plans and cycles layouts for the week. This process is fairly simple after all the planning that took place Monday through Wednesday, and I usually have it done before the Friday afternoon dismissal.

I take any time necessary during my planning period to organize or complete any last-minute PPOP tasks, then place the disciplines in their assigned locations at the TASK tower in order of lessons. Friday planning period, I will bind my actual plans for that day in a folder together for Monday only. Monday represents the first day of the week in terms of lessons. Depending on the discipline, one lesson opened on Monday may not be complete until Wednesday. Therefore, I don't need to go back to my math drawer, for example, until I am ready for lesson two. The same for the rest of the disciplines. The Monday folder is actually not a Monday folder, the folder houses the plans for that actual date. This way I am organized, reaching and shuffling in a dated folder instead of many pages and resources in a book. Everything is housed neatly, not falling and constantly having to be resorted. Once I've completed a lesson or the work for that date, what will be referenced again is stored; all else is returned into the unit binder or tossed in the kept recycle bin.

There you have it, PPOPed and PPOPed. PPOPed for the upcoming week and PPOPed completely for next lesson unit, lesson plans, small groups, rotations, grades, homework, objectives, warm-ups , handouts

and the morning messages. Super- Rockstar Star teacher status. Friday afternoons, after closing your classroom out, when you leave, walk out in peace and excitement. Be sure to take your lanyard off, you're done for the weekend.

CHAPTER 6

CHAPTER 6

"The Professional Triplets and Dynamics of Professionalism and Communication"

By now, we can say that you successfully know how to PPOP. PPOPing is key to successful classroom and workload management. However, this chapter is not about PPOPing – this chapter is about the sophistication. This chapter is going to focus on the steps for the sophisticated side of teaching with respect to PIG.

Your interactions are each uniquely your own experience. How you choose to receive and react to them are matters of choice. Your choices are greatly impacted by your mindset, emotional state, and degree of readiness at that time. Most of these things are far beyond the reach of my own control, but thankfully, all are completely and utterly yours.

Let's begin with our mentality. We will keep it simple, as always. There are two principles I preach.

"No matter how emotionally charged I am, please don't dismiss and trample over my emotions."

Even if nobody ever says it out loud, we all secretly are saying it. As a teacher, you are dealing with a diverse spectrum of people, from children sometimes younger than five to staff members sometimes

well into their sixties. You have parents from all backgrounds, each with their own beliefs and parenting styles. Then you have the various unspoken dynamics between staff members, not to mention these different layers and dynamics are all interwoven into the structure of each day. One person's problems tend to trickle over to a few other people's problems, especially if it's a problem that has to do with students. Almost anything that has to do with students seems to trickle over to the teacher's desk. If it is a big enough deal or a small one, before you know it, there is a whole team of people disrupted over one issue.

There are so many different people in so many different spaces in life it is no wonder we can sometimes feel the most comfortable closed up in our classrooms with our class and our own system of sanity (or *insanity*). No matter how you try to avoid it or where you hide, you will come across a "less than ideal" situation where someone is emotionally exploding their frustrations all over you. It is going to happen at least once with a parent, student, or staff member. Guess what? Surprise, you're going to do it to somebody too. And that's okay. We are all just ordinary people. John Legend made a whole song about it; you can add it to your morning drive playlist. We all make choices. We have all made great ones, poor ones and spontaneously, emotionally charged, without-thinking ones. I have always found it in my best interest to accept what I can accept and forget the rest. Before we begin, it is important to establish your professional principles for interactions.

PROFESSIONAL/PARAMOUNT PRINCIPLES

There are two professional principles I like to stand on when it comes to my interactions with staff, students, and stakeholders. The first:

humility, respect, and forgiveness. There is a simple rule, "Treat every-one in the way in which you want to be treated." Understanding that rule is the foundation of the first principle. I try to never forget that, no matter who the person is – their title, position, etc. I remember that the person standing in front of me is a person just like I am. I have my moments that are good and naughty too.

No matter if a person is treating you with kindness or harshness, respect them and their right to have a moment. Allow them the space to vent and release it, just as you would want someone to allow you if you were having a really harsh moment.

In short, principle one is I am human just like you, and I respect and forgive the humanness in you as I do in myself.

The second principle is to remember that teaching and learning are beyond the classroom. The entire school and staff are a part of your teaching resources and learning community. We are each connected to each other by the common goal of creating a safe and productive learning environment for the students. I always bring it back to that point. We are all here for the student's well-being and success. Think of the schoolhouse as one big ecosystem. Each entity is connected to the other, each contributing and impacting the other professionally, socially, and emotionally. We depend on each other for something at some time or another. We can unite, divide, support, and destroy each other without even knowing.

In short, the second principle is we are one big educational family. Cue Sister Sledge, "We are family. I love my school-wide commu-nity." I doctored the lyrics a bit, but that's another great one to add

to the playlist. Let's start with a few sophisticated tips for daily professional practices.

PROFESSIONAL PRACTICES, DUTIES, AND ROUTINES

These will be standard terminology and language, but for the sake of clarity, let's take a moment to break down the triplets of this chapter's title: the professional triplets refers to the three D's and S's of professional responsibilities and interactions we navigate day to day.

PROFESSIONALISM AND THE TRIPLE D'S

Professionalism is your work ethic. It is your code of honor and attitude, how you carry and maneuver yourself in and around the workplace. The term professionalism implies three things, all happening to begin with the letter D. The triple D's refer to dress, demeanor, and discourse. Think of professionalism as a role, and you are performing according to your part.

Take the triple Ds of a doctor to use as an example. If my profession is that of a pediatrician, I may wear a white lab coat and a stethoscope around my neck, but my demeanor is warming and friendly, and my discourse is simple and not overwhelming. The engagement with the patient should be different compared to that of an obstetrician, who may also wear a white lab coat, have a warming and friendly demeanor, and their discourse is not overwhelming, but it is specific and matter of fact.

The same logic should be applied to various roles and positions within the schoolhouse. The concept never seems to be a question for the P.E. teacher. No one questions the sweatpants and coaching demeanors because it all makes sense. If the P.E. teacher started wearing a suit or showing up in heels, then people may begin to inquire because then it doesn't make sense.

Does it make sense for a primary teacher to be decked to the nines in the traditional idea of professional clothes when they are working with children under the age of eight who often spill, make messes, and snag clothing? It may depend on demeanor and classroom management style. Should the intermediate teacher come to work in a slogan t-shirt and jeans? Maybe, again, triple D, that could depend on the teaching style and discourse they have with their students. The reasoning behind the triple D idea is that professionalism is not about how somebody dresses, speaks, or behaves – it's about all three of them and how they apply those to their job and the roles necessary to perform in their profession.

HALLWAY BEHAVIOR

Two key points to consider: you are 'on,' and smile.

In the hallway, you are on – on duty and on point. You are Mister or Miss so-and-so. Keep your professional face on in the hall. You never know who you could be walking by.

Always smile and greet your passing neighbor with words or a nod, but be sure to acknowledge everyone. It doesn't have to be an obnoxious hollering down the hallway, but a gentle wave or "good morning" to those you greet eyes with is always good practice.

APPLE BITE

The hallway can also be a phenomenal resource. When you can take time to take a personal tour around your school, observe the boards, the classroom dynamics, and learning. I have discovered some wonderful things along my hallway tours – some of them academic, but most of it being from how refreshing and rewarding it can be to wander the halls and see teachers teaching and students engaged in their learning. It really does warm the heart. That's a little educator's self-care tip; take an in-school vacation and travel down the hallways to refresh yourself. If nothing else, you get to feel like a rebel and be outside of your classroom while others are bound inside of theirs. I know that's immature and completely high school, but it still makes me smile.

GOSSIP VERSUS VENTING

Let's be honest, you are going to have days where one or two moments are going to test you. On one or two of those times, you are going to either pass or fail those challenges. Forgive yourself, reflect on the situation, and take away what will positively benefit you next time. Don't dwell on anything that is negative, even if you were the one who did it. With that said, keep the same in mind for the people you work with too.

Speaking harshly and unkindly about someone who angered or offended you is best done outside of the workplace and with non-work-associated people, period. I don't deny that you may have a moment, or somebody really did do an obnoxious and offensive action, but save the drama for your mama, literally. Literally call her up, a good girlfriend, or tell it to your front windshield as you are driving home from work. Words travel rapidly fast around the schoolhouse. Keep harsh words from your mouth out of it.

But if you ever find yourself at that moment where you just need to vent and you need to do it right now, be sure it is with that one, and only one, trusted colleague that you can count on to listen to you without over-giving their opinion and influence. Sometimes, it is really comforting to hear that cosigning, "I feel the same way too." But it can easily slip into a dumping fest of gossip. Venting is getting it all out an off your chest. Gossip is similar – with a pungent twist.

Avoid gossip. Read that again: avoid gossip, even with that trusted friend. It truly is gross. You will hear it regardless, but try your best to be an uninterested ear and walk past the water cooler crowd in the staff lounge. Stay focused on your agenda. Anything that you are supposed to know about you will. It will come directly to you. Stay focused, no worries.

DUTIES AND ROUTINES

Pickups, drop-offs, and duty post – this is a short a simple one to say; be on time always. There is no need to get into the various duties, as they vary per school and position. For pick-ups and drop-offs, I am primarily speaking of picking up and dropping off your class to the cafeteria, specials, the library, or periods where you are exchanging the responsibility of your class with someone else.

Time is valuable and precious when we are speaking of instruction. Your instructional and professional time is just as valuable as the next person's. Being late can be a fire-starter for some people. It does not matter how you view their use of their time – it matters to them. You can have compassion for and respect their time as you would want them to respect yours, even better than you would treat your own. Accept and forgive them when they take that time back intentionally or unintentionally at some point too. With this being said, I must provide a disclaimer.

DISCLAIMER

Alright, honesty hour. That last one is one that I tend to be inconsistent with. I tend, rather, I can be late for pick-ups. I know this is terrible. The time managing, system of efficacy for everything teacher is insufficiently late herself. Yes, this one is true and even worse a small part of it can even be in protest. I'm not turning my back on the system; this one has some personal ties. Please let me explain; it's time for a short story.

While I love teaching and deeply respect the profession, a part of me despises how overlooked it can sometimes feel when there have not been sufficient structures put into place for practitioners to thrive. Success is one thing, and thriving is another. For the majority of my career, my planning time has been distributed into the time before school, some time after dismissal, and a consistent thirty-minute period at some point for specials throughout the course of the day.

I will skip over the fact that thirty minutes for instructional planning is not the ideal amount of time desired and jump straight to my matters of protest. Within that same thirty-minute period is included the time to walk students to their destination, dropping them off, and return to pick them up. Within this same amount of time is the window you are expected, should you need to, to use the restroom, check your mailbox, email for updates, and do any classroom planning or instructional planning that needs to be done.

Needless to say, the time managing system for everything teacher is zapping, soaking, and absorbing every minute of that time down to the second. My protest comes in the form of, "I'm just using every bit of my time for the planning and little for the transporting." This is no excuse for poor behavior, and I am not promoting poor practice either. But those were a part of my reasonings why. Refereeing back to principles one and two: I am a person, and I sometimes throw tantrums too.

I would also like to include, should any one of the phenomenal support staff and specialist team members I happen to be late to pickups for be reading, this is my formal apology. I thank you for your grace and forgiveness. I am sorry. I know your time is valuable.

THE EMAIL

This section wouldn't be complete without a word on email. I got some of the best advice on how to handle emails from a very good friend and teammate of mine one year in fifth grade. Her words were very simple. In fact, it was one word: "delete." It took me years to finally understand and master this.

Once I did, things changed for me. Delete. It is that simple. In my district, we use a Gmail platform, and Gmail allows you to make folder tag categories for emails you do not want to see in your inbox. It is also connected to google docs, where various formations of documents can be stored electronically.

When incoming emails enter my inbox, I start each morning by addressing the immediate deletes because they are the most fun – any advertisements, promotions, or things I know I have no interest in or how they got my email, I delete.

Next, I try to open and address that morning any emails from parents as soon as possible, even if it is just to say I will be returning with a response. That response I save for rare occasions; otherwise, I try to address right them then and there.

Next would be staff emails with updated information. I read and jot down anything that needs to be remembered and that I do not intend to return to. On the side of my Gmail layout, I have folders designated for specific information and things. I keep it simple: parent communication and contact dated for that school year, staff information dated for that school year (usually deleted at the end of the school year), a folder dedicated to information regarding our grade level specifically, and a save folder for miscellaneous emails and things to be saved.

Everything else gets printed, saved, or deleted. All things related to the school that are important and should be saved are stored in the google docs for accessing and filing.

Keeping a clean email will give you direction each day in what and who to respond to. It also is extraordinarily rewarding when you can delete a whole page and see absolutely nothing. For emails that enter throughout the day, make it a point to check once after lunch or specials for any midday updates from the administration about dismissal changes, etc., and then not again until the end of the day after dismissal when you will clear out your email for the day. After a certain time – for me, it is once I leave the school building – no longer respond or check emails again until returning to school the following day. Check three times, respond twice, and keep your inbox clean.

UNSPOKEN DYNAMICS

It is ironic that I am using the term unspoken when I am well aware these dynamics are spoken plenty about in gossip discussions. I use "unspoken" because these dynamics are undercurrents of the school atmosphere that almost everybody feels and knows about, but very few are often clarified or addressed.

We will discuss staffing transitions and promotions further in Chapter 8, but until then, when it comes to the topic of the hiring and staffing positions dynamics, who has what position? How did they get it, and how well are they doing in it? I can answer those questions in a single sentence: none of your concern. Follow the same ideas as gossip and venting. Mind your own business; this will yield much value.

Another unspoken dynamic is the 'work buddies' dynamics. I do not protest friendships or working relationships, but when it comes to work, specifically 'school' work, we are colleagues, not classmate friends. Genuine chemistry can't be hidden, but really challenge yourself to ask if the chemistry is productive or destructive.

You can always spend time and share stories after work hours, but if the bulk of your time together is spent sharing stories and gossip, you may have a classmate friend and not a colleague. This goes beyond

being able to work and talk. Can we plan and produce outcomes together? Are we discussing problem-solving and solution-oriented ideas, or is this just an opportunity to share my complaints with somebody else? You set the tone for the types of working relationships you want to accept. After that, it is their choice whether or not they decide to be on board.

PROFESSIONAL UPLIFT

The opposite end of discerning working relationships is fostering them. This is where we discuss some of the fun things. We discussed the core principles and how we are all people too. Well, I don't know about you, but if I am sticking with principle one, I like to know I matter from time to time and am cared for.

The simplest and most effective thing you can do to positively impact yourself is to tell people thank you when you truly mean it. Say it when you don't too, and your gratitude will catch up. The next thing you can do is support, not just offer support, but actually support them when they need it.

Check in from time to time on another staff member that is not a part of your team. Yes, you should check on teammates as well, but it is even more meaningful to reach over to that teacher in primary or intermediate you rarely see beyond the sign-in sheet and staff meetings. You get to pop in, check out another grade, refresh your practice, and build professional relationships that are authentic and valuable even if you never utilize the value. Don't go searching for someone to befriend with the expectation of asking them for a favor later, and especially do not go doing that with teachers. Teachers talk, and you do not want to receive that label. It can be hard to recover from. A simple "Hey, how are you doing? I noticed your grade was working on such and such. My grade is too," or an "I heard of a strategy you use that works really well. Could I stop by during one of my specials to watch a snippet of your lesson?" is perfecrt.

This can be an intimidating one, but if your PIG is true, you should be fine; go for it, and don't forget to thank them for allowing you to observe and spend some of their time. However, I may not begin with this one. A meaningful class or instructional compliment to break the ice will suffice in the beginning. While it is our natural tendencies to give superficial compliments to begin introductions, remember you are not sowing seeds for work buddies; you are sowing seeds for working relationships with a colleague. You set the tone with the topic of your interests.

Okay, those were some simple ways to uplift collogues – meaningful thank you's and compliments. Let's get into some fun ways!

When I can and it is fitting, I like to pump my thank you's up a notch. I honor the authentic *thank you* in the moment, but later, I like to send my *victims* a thank you card. Now rarely has this backfired on me, but it has knowingly at least once, so I will say that knowing your audience and the delivery is very important. But for the most part, this tip is a winner.

I keep a set of blank thank you cards in my desk drawer and some confetti. When I want to send one of my thank you's, I send them a card with a written message filled with confetti. This part is the key!

Once I fill the card, I place it upside down in the envelope, so when the *victim* pulls their card out, they receive a thank you and a small blast of confetti. A *popping* surprise! (I couldn't resist the pun.) I have since learned to warn people not to open over food. It is completely silly, and most have told me it was a warranted surprise that took them right back to childhood days of celebrations. Sometimes, I'll sprinkle a bit of confetti on their work chair or desk for them to see when they return to work the next day because why not?

For support staff, I try to make it a habit to have the students they work with support them on their birthdays with a thank you card and some confetti or a piece of candy too. I think it is important to remind people that they do matter and what they are doing is important. Now don't go overdoing it. Your building supervisor will have a fit, and you are probably no longer utilizing your time wisely.

THE TRIPLE S'S: STAFF, STUDENTS, AND STAKEHOLDERS

It should be standard language, but for the sake of clarity, let's take a moment to break down the three S's: staff, students, and stakeholders.

Staff includes all working members of the school building from the county maintenance you only see when they are called in to fix the big problems to the county superintendent or CEO of schools – every working member that in some manner contributes to the working and success of your school building can be considered 'staff'. Staff is everybody in the building and everybody working for the same organization outside of it.

The term "students" understandably refers to the students of your classroom, as well as every other student in the building. Consider each and every student, child, and sibling that walks in and out of that building as a student of your own. If they are young enough, you never know, they may really end up being yours.

Stakeholder is a term I did not become fluent with until I began graduate school. Stakeholder sounds so businessy and professional, doesn't it? Well, it is; never forget this is a profession, and to a degree, it is also a business. In the business of education, the parents and community are your customers and student outcomes your product. Having parent or community buy-in to support, sponsor, or promote the school or that phenomenal teacher loving their job and letting it shine through in a rapid way is so important. Alright, wonderful – we have established our common understanding of each term. Let's dive in!

STAFF

We can preach all good things, but realistically, everyone you encounter is not going to have the same degree of or respect for professionalism that you may. There are some people who you see that look like they don't work at all. There are others you may see that look like they are working entirely too hard. Remember that through both lenses that is only what you *see*. Don't judge, and don't worry. Don't worry about being the one who does all the work or fear that something catastrophic will fall apart because somebody else did not do something they said they would do. All things do work out. Focus instead on remaining consistent in good work ethic and being intentional and putting your best efforts forth in the work that you are doing.

Consistency will show itself, and you will stand on your own. You don't have to suffer because your teammates suck or feel insecure because you think your teammates are better or superior in practice than you are. Focus on yourself and your own professional goals. Continue to model through your character, your principles, and your passion for the profession. Be gentle in judgment and receptive to the flow of faith. All good things will come to those that are consistently acting in good. Relax and look straight.

However, it would not be my due diligence if I did not share with you a few types of staff members you may encounter along the way and how to navigate working with or around them. They are not exclusive to age but to character and behavior. To begin, I would like to state that these are just types of personalities and habits I have noticed along my way. These are some of the most popular themes I have come across but are not inclusive of everyone. You may or may not find yourself amongst any. I am sure you may have at least seen one or two. These are also not classifications of good versus bad; these are just descriptions.

TYPES OF STAFF

SUPER TEACHERS

The super teacher is somewhere along the lines of Ms. Frizzle from *The Magic School Bus* or Ms. Honey from *Matilda*. They are, by all accounts, perfect. They have the best rooms with the cutest designs and pieces. They have the best boards with cute borders and themes. They always have their stuff turned in, usually first, and it's always great. They always have things to share and say about their parents and students. They are usually current and up to date with the latest technology and trends.

Sounds like the ideal teacher, right? Well, you are not wrong. The super teacher usually does sound like the ideal teacher. But remember looks can be deceiving – not always, but they can be.

Take one moment and reflect on your day-to-day practices as a classroom teacher. Okay, now think about when in your day-to-day you have time for things that would put you on the status of Miss Frizzle or Ms. Honey – super teacher. Now take a moment and reflect on your superstar colleague and ask yourself: how early are they arriving and late are they staying each day? If the answer is not before and after me, almost every day but Friday, then ask yourself this next question: when do they find the time to do all these superstar things and still teach?

They usually don't. I'm being honest. This isn't theory – it's often, unfortunately, fact. I have found it to be true, time and time again. Teachers who appear to be super and have the best rooms and strive to be the superstar most of the time usually have more than a few things to hide.

A simple rule of logic my father taught me as a child was, "If it doesn't make sense, it doesn't make sense." Literally, if it does not make sense, or if it could not even be possible within the information known, it is usually because it is complete nonsense. Here's one for security purposes – ask yourself the questions that don't make sense and sensibly answer them. When do they have time to cut out every piece of material for every single thing that they do? During the school day? During the times when they should be teaching? It is not always

true; some super teachers put in the long hours and work it takes, but remember this is not about judgment, just insight.

Insight: Do not waste your time comparing yourself to others. There is often more or far less to the story than what meets the eyes. You may find that these super teachers never seem to be that super when it comes to sharing tips, ideas, time, anything. They can be very vague when it comes to the specifics of how they get to the core of their superness, yet they tend to be very loud with the details of how super they are. So again, do not worry or fret if you ever work with or be inspired by one of such. Oftentimes, the super teacher is the super phony teacher- but not always.

HERMIT CRAB TEACHERS

The hermit crab teacher takes emphasis on the hermit, likes to work independently and focus on their class, their classroom, and maintaining good work ethics overall. This type of teacher usually is not super concerned about being the best but doing their best job. They have a strong work ethic, and they don't say much or protest publicly or even privately. They're more likely to agree to or get negotiated into doing things they probably did not want to do or would have done a different way had they felt comfortable to speak up.

The opposite side of the hermit crab teacher focuses on the crab. There may be a withdrawn, passive-aggressive involvement style with a tiny bit of negativity to them. They may also enjoy watching public protest and participate privately. This crabby teacher's perspective of independence may be to go completely rogue and against the grain.

They may also prefer to maintain a subtle profile to mask or deflect from things that may not really be getting done with fidelity.

Insight: The hermit crab teacher is the one to be mindful of. There is usually great knowledge and a wealth of experience and information to be shared, but they are not going to share willingly with just anyone. If you stepped into their classroom, you would probably find an organized and very peaceful environment because those qualities are probably strongly desired by this type of teacher.

They may or may not do well with behavior management, and conflict resolution might not be the strongest tool in their kit. The conflict with this type of teacher is that they may be overly passive when it comes to operating as a team and making decisions or overly defensive when confronted. A tip for navigating this type of person is to build a genuine one-on-one relationship with them first. Value their perspectives, and take your time. Don't overdo it – a hermit crab usually likes its space.

THE VETS

The vets are your veteran teachers, but the term is not exclusive to age. The vets are your tenured teachers for sure but also the ones with the effortless confidence – the confidence gained from being confirmed in their practice, sure of their ability and ability to adapt and cope with change. They are a large part of the school culture and discourse, vocally or internally. Vet teachers tend to be your shakers and doers in whatever it is they are doing. They know how to take risks and can be comfortable taking them within reason. Instructionally, vets tend to

focus on programs and instruction that are student-centered and less teacher-directed.

Insight: The vets are great teachers to learn from and build relationships with. They are usually confident and knowledgeable in the profession and have had great experiences to share. They also usually have the best stories are great conversationalist. When working and interacting with these types of teachers, know that they can sometimes be stubborn. That is usually from the tried and truly tested patience they have had to spare developing their profession and practice over the years. They also tend to be the ones with the best connections. Maybe it's the level-headedness and people skills or years put in, but they usually know everybody from the guy who comes in quarterly to restock the vending machine to the attendance and payroll secretaries at the board.

NEW TEACHERS AND OLD

The new teachers and old teachers, in general, are contrasting opposites but uniquely the same. The new teacher, whether young in age or new in career, is usually very ambitious and willing to suggest and do everything. They can be a pain in the staff meeting because they are always raising their hand and volunteering the team to do something or raising their hand and sharing an optimistically naive opinion.

The old teacher, whether old in career or old in passion, is usually underwhelmingly uninvolved and willing to negate or suggest options for almost everything. They can be a pain in the staff meeting because it is hard to hear over their negative side chatter or because they have

126

a drastic one-in-a-million chance scenario to share an opposing option for every decision made.

Insight: In both circumstances, take a back seat. Let them have the wheel and be strategic in how and when to interest yourself. The new teacher's ideas may seem far-fetched, but with tailoring and some more research, the idea may be godsent! Equally, an old teacher's method may seem out of date, but with an update, they are exactly the strategy you needed to overcome. In the midst of the two spectrums, you may find it easier to just check yourself out. Instead, take a back seat, enjoy the ride, and utilize your listening ears for the commonalities and resolutions.

THE WONDER TEACHERS

I have a favorite thing in each chapter, and in this chapter this group description might be it. The wonder teachers are one of my favorite groups to utilize my hallway behavior skills on. That's smile, greet, and keep on walking. Notice it does not say wonderful. The wonder teachers are the magicians of the group. They are the most magical in their manipulative and maneuvering ways. These teachers are the ones you ask yourself in wonder, "Hey, I wonder what they do? I wonder when they do what it is that they do? I wonder how they are able to get away with that?" Seriously, I would be stressed. I am not the type to enjoy sitting around idle doing nothing or finding ways to manipulate myself out of doing something. I would get anxiety if I lived my days every day having to fight that fight.

Be mindful of this type because they come in all forms and can be quite sophisticated and elusive. They may show themselves as lazy

or helpless, manipulating you to pick up the pieces. Or they could be extra friendly and wanting to be your absolute best friend for no apparent reason. They over-indulge in the flattery and compliments, but later on, they are usually looking for a favor.

One of the tricks they use is their trick of unavailability. They may have mastered the power of invisibility by always being willing to run an errand or fill in for someone or something else beyond their duty or to conveniently later use this as the reasoning as to why they could not fulfill their responsibility. "Oh, lunch duty? Emergency pullout? I had to cover such and such..." Right.

Insight: Do not be flustered by this type. There is usually an underlying reasoning behind these tactics, and you usually want nothing to do with them. That includes know-how about them. Instead of focusing on how irritating it can be to count on somebody who is never there, do not count on them. You can plan with them intentionally and prepare them so that they know to be present and that this will be expected or keep a simple record on display, transparently identifying these moments for the purpose of tracking and record-keeping. If it is someone who is a specialist avoiding their services or a support staff that diligently eludes their duty, they are usually assigned for a purpose and to specific students or student needs for a reason, sometimes mandated. Rarely are people in the classroom just because.

Therefore, if you decided to keep a record, remember it is for tracking and record-keeping purposes only. You are not anyone's boss. Check yes, they were present. Place an X if they were not. It's up to them and administration to justify where the person was and who gave who permission, etc. You are just documenting services and support received or unreceived. Resist the urge to be a clock stalker. Check they were there. X they were not. Slash they came in, stayed for ten minutes, and walked out. No need for the nineteen minutes and thirty-two seconds record keeping. You don't have time for that.

MEETINGS, CONFERENCES, AND PROFESSIONAL DEVELOPMENTS

When it comes to how to behave and interact, that's simple – professionally with sophistication and intention. When in doubt, PIG it out. Remember what your purpose for being present is, the intentions you want to receive and demonstrate, or how to pursue the goals you are hoping to achieve from being there when they are addressed. Meetings, conferences, and professional developments can be long and boring, especially if the presenter is not entertaining or your motivation for attendance was less than your own. Just PIG out and be present in the moment.

For the other half, the information, I keep it super simple. I prefer a notebook to a running document; you should specify your preference. I grab one composition notebook with an interesting color or cover, usually green or pink, so that it stands out to others. I label it with my name, school, and use. That is it. One journal for meetings. I write the date and title or host of the meeting at the top (staff meeting, team meeting, etc.) and the intention. Bullet point any key ideas and circle all important dates. To take it up a notch, in the front cover, I write a simple key out for sticky notes and highlights.

I tend to use blue, standout pink, and resource green. Blue sticky notes and highlights represent information I intend to return back to. Pink symbolizes standout ideas or things that are really "hot" topic and priority to me. Green stickies or highlights symbolize resources. Things that I could use, may want to use, or look into researching later. The yellow highlighter is for highlighting anything else important. After a meeting, I will take a moment to review the information received and decide if there is anything I want to note and if so which color. That's it.

Professional developments and meetings usually come with minute notes or an agenda detailing the information. The notebook is just for me and my take always. I write on the right front side of the page only and the left side (backside of the previous page) I leave for later ideas and questions I intend to be returning to later with answers. I keep this process until the end of the school year. When the end of the school year arrives, I take a mini binder clip and clip that year's pages to the front page. Then I take two pages, fold them into a triangular dividing tab and label it for the next school year. In the next school year, I use that same journal for the same information. I will continue this process until the journal ends. I try to be smart, and if the journal has seven pages left and probably will not make it through the next school year, I close it out and store it away for reference. Then I begin a new journal.

For conferencing, specifically parent-and-student conferences, not to be mistaken with the call log, I maintain the same journal routine, but the format changes a little. Each initial conference begins the same – the front page is dedicated to the student, and several pages are skipped, about five pages, for other things – not only for follow up conferencing but a reflection page too. The parent conference journal conferences are separated by triangular tabs labeled for the students. I also limit the color red. Red is the only color pen that does not get used casually. Red is saved for concrete agreed-upon statements. If it is written in red, it is usually a follow-up to something that has been changed or completed. I date all updates in this journal. Rarely has the degree of severity I put into the system for using this journal been needed to be used, thankfully. However, just in case, it is better to have it written down and dated.

STUDENTS

There are complete series and thousands of books, even studies, on how to manage student behavior and interactions. I could even write one, through my lens, but this section is not about that. This book is about you and for you, educators, the teacher. This section is about students from a general standpoint.

STUDENT INFORMATION

When it comes to student information, I maintain similar principles for them as I do for me. I found the best results in simplicity and simplifying the general way to navigate students, focusing on student expectations, managing student behaviors, and student information.

Student information is kept and stored in one binder. Take the time to develop it; choose a standout color – I chose red. Include all general student information including health, data, grades, special informa-

tion, and any extracurricular or clubs they are a part of. This makes it super easy when it comes time to grab things for meetings – simple meeting journal, laptop, red binder, and pen. If I needed student samples, I grab them as necessary and keep a few key samples included with each student intended for the meeting. This is not a slim and sleek binder. It was sleek and thick.

STUDENT EXPECTATIONS

The expectations for the students are simple and based on three things: respect, kindness, and safety. I model the same behaviors through my interaction with students and staff and am always sure to implement these same three principles into the culture of student-to-student interactions.

The second expectation is that they greet me each day at the door before they enter the classroom. Again, there are books and studies on this. I could even explain my own, but that would be a book chapter on its own. So, let's just say it gently encourages respect, confidence, and manners. It sets the tone and allows for a quick informal assessment of each student's potential mood, injuries, and a quick moment to interact with them on a non-instructional basis.

The third expectation is that my students bring and present their best in all that they do. Whatever their best is, bring it, and bring it well. I ask that they bring their best for themselves and bring their best for their peers as well. It is a part of our class culture to bring our best efforts, whatever they may be at the time.

The final principle is feedback. Take the time to establish a culture of positive and constructive feedback among students. This helps in directing their discourse toward being academic and constructive. It will promote an honest and safe environment for learning. Being intentional with feedback and requiring students to give and receive feedback also aids in academic ownership and responsibility.

Finally, for myself, I make it a point to encourage my students to utilize their academic environment. In addition to classroom jobs, they are not chained or expected to stay in their seats at all times. They can work with or alongside peers on the carpet or any of the other learning areas. Allowing students to feel comfortable and free to move about the classroom encourages ownership and responsibility for their environment.

STAKEHOLDERS: PARENT, COMMUNITY, AND COMMUNICATION

Okay, I have heard some contend that parents can be the grizzly bears of teaching, but that is just one way of looking at it. Parents can also be some of your greatest assets. They can be your support system and your direct line to students when you are intentional about building positive relationships with them. They can be the greatest care bears too.

If it is not apparent by now, I like to create purpose, intentions, and goals in most of what I do. I once received some very purposeful and intentional words as a student from my mentor teacher. It was my very first parent-teacher conference day ever, and we had gone through several different emotional expressions and experiences with parents. I looked at her, and I asked her how she was able to handle it. How could she handle the emotion and face-to-face pressure of a parent and tell them the truth, for better or worse – better easier of course – about their child? Her response was to remember that no matter what it may look like to us, that parent is giving us their very best. That student is their great gift, joy, achievement, and hope. We only have them for a glimpse of time; this is their baby forever. Be honest, be straight, and be gentle.

I'll admit that at the time I thought the remarks were sentimental, and I knew that they had merit, but I didn't quite get it yet. She knew that because her follow-up response was that I would see things differently once I had my own children. I haven't had my own child yet, but I have since gained the value of her words.

I believe she said it best, but to reiterate, there isn't a parent out there that decided to intentionally send their kid to school to do their worst, act out, and by all standards attempt to ruin your day. Never take it personally. Remember you and that parent are on the same team, team "let's get this young scholar to successfully grow academically and gain skills they need to achieve as they progress through life."

Be gentle and forgiving with parents. Forget what you heard about them, and try to walk into each new meeting with a warm and accepting greeting. This year is a new opportunity to write a new story.

From a general sense, over my career, I have found three common themes of things most parents care about: Are you doing your job? Is my kid safe? How is my kid doing? There are some that care about the circumstances of the other students, but usually, it's a singular thought. Be proactive and address the primary concerns first. The overarching theme is communication. Sending a progress note or shout-out email spontaneously for those student families that you may not be in communication with often are great thoughts as well.

ACADEMIC COMMUNICATION AND FEEDBACK

Communicate through a monthly or quarterly newsletter that highlights what has taken place, student achievement, what's to come, and some information about the class or school culture to address the general audience inquiry. Keep it simple. The majority of the information you will be pulling from your district curriculum. In my school district, there are already pre-made descriptions and homework help for parents made for each science and math unit. We can print and send them home. To keep it simple, assign a simple word definition or problem from the newsletter or unit description as a parent homework over the weekend as a reading incentive.

Parents want to know how their child is doing. Make it a habit to reach out to them routinely. Making a phone call or writing out an email each time can be time-consuming. Writing a short note such as "Superstar Participation Today" is simple, quick, rewarding, and specific to why the student is being praised. The hope is that the parent will ask their child what they participated in, and the student can share what took place that school day. Completed assignments should be going home each week. Within that pile of assignments, choose at least one or two that include authentic feedback, whether it is feedback on progress or improvement. Requiring students to return that example with a parent response or feedback to initial the feedback suggestions made creates meaning and a PIG for that feedback to be used.

RESPECT THE PIG

Respect the PIG. PIG will keep you focused in action and focused in work. Here are some simplified tips for interacting and communicating with parents.

- Keep it timed. A golden rule for a one-on-one meeting is under thirty minutes. If you are meeting with a parent in front of a team, that is different. Having a timeframe allows you to exit if the meeting is unproductive, dragging, or heating up and return at a later date.

1. If a meeting is losing focus, bring back the PIG. Refocus the meeting; restructure so that the meeting topic and content are focused on achieving the intended goal. The intentions of the meeting are always to identify and/or develop the steps to achieve the goal. Remember that the goal is always the success of the student. When in doubt, PIG it out.

2. Finally, record and document everything. It is never about trying to catch or build a case up against someone. It should not have to be about protecting yourself, but it is – protecting your right to forget a detail and protecting yourself against what was and was not said. It is also for resource and reference purposes.

One for good measure: make it a point to remember that in order to teach, you must learn. Try never to fall victim to the educator's ego syndrome. No matter if it is with an adult or a student, it is never an error to have a flaw or make a mistake. A school is supposed to be a learning environment and not a learning institution. As a teacher, we are not expected to know everything, but we are expected to have the ability to resource the tools and knowledge to find out. To keep it simple, if you make a mistake or error and a parent points it out, thank the parent and remember to always value the teamwork and appreciate the second set of eyes. It is not personal; it is professional. Mistakes and errors happen. Be diligent and prompt in correcting them and grateful for the opportunity to not make another.

CHAPTER 7

CHAPTER 7

"Clock in, Clock out"
– Home, Work, Life, and Balance

To teach is to serve. A teacher is someone who services and attends to others. It is one of the most beautiful things about teaching, and I believe what keeps us all here is the personal rewards we gain from servicing our students and communities. It goes without saying that teachers, especially elementary teachers, will and do go far above the call of duty when it comes to their students and their classrooms.

In addition to that, teaching can be a "takeover" job. It can take over your life, your health, your relationship, and monopolize your time if you are not careful. At some point, that duty of being a constant giver and little receiver begins to take a toll on the body, the mind, and the spirit. As teachers and as professionals, when we establish our non-negotiables and know what our priorities are, it is a lot simpler to define and respect our boundaries between work and home.

This chapter is not about cutting things out or finding the time to meditate and do yoga each morning before work. Although those routines would be nice, this is about managing your priorities and maintaining your peace of mind and joy. In this chapter, we will focus on

what will be your two top priorities from now on – prioritizing balance and professional self-care.

BALANCE

Balance is a simple idea but tricky action. To balance, you have to be intentional and disciplined. It is not something that just poof, or PPOP – see what I did there – appears overnight. It is something you stumble with at first, fall off a few times, then one day while taking similar actions as before, somehow, wow, you got it! With consistency, it becomes easier and easier to maintain. Personal balance is the same. Balancing your work life against your personal life is the same game. The only difference is we tend to let the demands of our work life outweigh the demands of our personal life. It's alright at first. Balance is a back and forth game, but when the weight of the work life far outweighs that of home and personal life, no matter what the reward, our worlds are out of balance, and we will begin to suffer the costs. Physical health, relationships, happiness, emotional health, our diet, our skin, and hair become impacted by our moods. It's a very unpretty effect of imbalance, which is why balance is key.

There are a ton of angels and several different things you can focus on when it comes to work life home life balance. We are going to focus on balancing our time and balancing our energy.

TIME

We discussed how to plan and how to PPOP when it comes to work-load management. Mastering that skill will be key in being able to move forward successfully into work and home balance. Being able to master your time and remain consistent with your planning schedules is how you begin to master the work/life side of work and home balance. Our goal is to be able to successfully complete our workload within our work hours and be able to leave work each day with that day's duties completed and our next day prepped. There is no homework or even a need to take a workbag back and forth, but we will talk about the workbag a bit more when we discuss professional self-care.

Some can do it, but I have found little success in actually sticking to the rule of never ever taking things home and only working within my work hours. I have tried, and I continue to say that realistically there really is not enough time allotted in the day to complete everything. Inevitably, there is some time that must be committed outside the work hours. This time is precious time. This is never to be forgotten that this is your time. Take this time with the thought in mind, "This time is my precious and sacred teaching time. This time is for (insert your purpose), and when I am working during my sacred time I am planned, I am prepared, I am organized, and I will be able to productively execute. This time is extra special time from me to me."

Each day, commit one hour or forty-five minutes of additional work time to your school day just to ensure you are not frantically working and have time to get everything done. Be smart and be balanced in how you divide this extra time. According to my personal work schedule, I try to arrive thirty minutes earlier consistently in the morning. In the afternoons, I complete that time by leaving fifteen minutes after work. For my current school schedule, I am expected to arrive by 8:30 a.m.

which means arriving at 8:00 a.m. for my thirty-minute mornings and working until 4:15 p.m. for the fifteen-minute afternoons.

The best time to arrive is early because most people do not; it is usually much quieter, and you are a bit fresher in the morning. I have found only the first two to be true for me. I actually tend to be a bit slower in the morning; therefore, my morning tasks are usually not things that are going to require an enormous amount of brain energy, similar to my afternoons. However, the bounty that can be found in carving out morning time has been glorious. This schedule works Monday through Thursday, but Fridays are different. The bell dismisses everyone at the same time on Fridays.

During the week, in the afternoon, try to commit between ten to fifteen minutes after work each day, and on one afternoon a week, make the commitment to spend at least thirty minutes after school. Rarely do I spend over an hour. The time between student dismissal and the time we are contractually complete for the day is thirty minutes, so I make sure to spend that time PPOP-ing. The extra ten to fifteen minutes in the afternoon is primarily for sending your clearing emails, ensuring that boards are prepared for the next day, washing your hands, watering the plant, and saying good evening to any remaining coworkers. It's time to walk out the door without rush or worry, the room ready for your smooth arrival when you return.

Establishing personal workday hours is key in maintaining balance. Set those professional work hours and stick to them like glue. That is the best time to work. You are no longer defined by the clock. It's important to put time in and to have time out not only for balance but for creativity and mental rest. You will have greater longevity as a professional when you are not exhausted or depleted by the efforts you are committing to your career when you make sure you are putting effort elsewhere too.

When it comes to balancing your work and personal life, establish a professional work hour schedule that you are committed to keeping and can actually maintain. Do not set a work schedule crazy early like 6:15 a.m. or say you are going to stay late each afternoon. I've been there and failed at that. Learn from my failure and develop your next success. Make sure the schedule is one that is realistic and one you can keep. If you're an early bird, an early six a.m. schedule and zero minutes after work may be what works best for you. If you need more time at home or for other responsibilities in the morning, then as early as you can, consistency is what you are aiming for. In the afternoons, I recommend distinguishing additional work hours, and I use a timer set for fifteen minutes to stay on track. However, I generally spend about ten minutes of overtime. The extra five or ten minutes usually come by matter of clearing my desk, grabbing my belongings, walking down the hallway, and traveling across the parking lot to my car door.

Once you get your professional work schedule down, then each week take some time to make a draft plan your workweek PPOP planning schedule for the coming week. There is an example of how to PPOP your workweek in Chapter 5. This way, each morning when you are coming into work, including Monday, you know what you will be doing during this time period. You will have your work hours set and how you will manage your workload over the coming workweek. This

will aid you in balancing your work and home life before you commit yourself to completing your work within the time given and you have established a boundary of time to do it within.

PPOP ahead, of course. I am not going to advocate or discriminate against waking up early or earlier to have more time in the morning. It is a beautiful thing when I have extra time in the morning to complete my routines. But naturally, I am a night owl, and I prefer to work and be active in the night. I enjoy the night immensely. There is something so satisfying about those wee hours in the night when the whole world is quiet and it's just me, the moon, and my thoughts. I probably experience the same joy early risers experience when they rise at the hours of four and six a.m.; except for me, it is usually between midnight and two.

I have tried and tried. You can ask my parents; they have tried too. Getting to bed early is just something I have never naturally done. So, waking up earlier than I already do each morning is not a realistic idea for me which is why I don't push the whole early-riser thing on anyone. If you can do it, great. I admire you. If you can't do it, great. I am similar to you.

Plan and prepare your lunches and outfits ahead of time. I am not someone who can decide on a Sunday everything I will be wearing and how for the next five days, but I can iron and prep the clothes I think I may reach for in advance and have them ready to grab. I tend to stick with a basic wardrobe theme each week. Mondays, I want something very professionally styled. Tuesday through Thursdays, I like to keep it simple with one thing to put on and do dress and tights or skirts, and Fridays, I have no preference. Establish your flow. You know you will need lunch every day, so pack one or incorporate the time to pick up one in advance, but bring a lunch that you are going to look forward to. Lunchtime can be one of the few times you get to have to yourself. Enjoy the moment with a simple treat at least once a week.

PROFESSIONAL SELF-CARE

People talk about self-care and personal care, but not often are the two terms – professional and self-care – used together, especially when in the teaching profession. This is because I am convinced nobody ever seriously considers it. Well, in this chapter, we will.

I will divide this section on self-care into two segments, the work-week self-care practices that should be practiced professionally and self-care practices for the profession in general.

THE WORKWEEK

Once you have set your professional work hours, do not go outside of those hours. You have already committed additional time that was of your own to the job. Be satisfied and content. Know that you have committed yourself to doing your best during those times, and be at peace. When the bell rings to go home, release. There is one rule for after work and three things to remember to maintain it. The rule is no homework. Do not bring anything home that is related to work. Don't do it. You are not doing it. Do not do it. No homework.

To maintain that rule, there are three things to master. First, leave your workbag at work. If there is a time that you have scheduled after work that is a part of your professional work hour schedule, then on that one day okay. The rest of the week, leave it at school. It can come home on Fridays if you are the type that likes to have things just in case or look things over on the weekend. We will discuss work on the weekends in a moment. But other than that, nope. Get comfortable with walking into work with your purse, your lunchbox, your work keys, and hard drive. Walk confidently, and let your shoulders and arms breathe. No workbag toting to and from. Let the workbag security blanket go. There is no need to bring your workbag anyway; you do not do schoolwork at home.

The second is ensuring that you close out your classroom before you leave each afternoon. Do not leave things undone. Follow the rules for leaving the classroom each day. Be sure to have the satisfaction in deleting your emails, clearing your desk, and washing your hands before you walk out the door.

These last three tasks are your steps for completing, clearing, and closing your room each afternoon. Once these steps are complete, turn out the lights and walk away. You have made sure your room is ready, your plans and lessons are PPOPed, and you know what you are doing when you walk into the room the next morning. Walk away. Your job is done. You do not need to take anything home with you. Anything that was not completed you have already planned time for completing at some point within your week. Walk away satisfied. "I can go home I am finished for today."

The third is actually my favorite – no grading papers at home. At some point, you may have to bend the rules on this one. And if you do, that is alright. There are usually four quarters within a school year, so allow yourself four one-assignment-only homework passes. The reason the name is one-assignment instead of home time is that this is a super emergency card you are using to break a foundational key to the rule of no homework. The term one-assignment is used because if you have to use this card you may need more than one evening, maybe a weekend, to complete it. Sometimes that happens; that's life, and that can sometimes be the demand of any profession. So, use that one assignment card, and use the time needed to complete it. Once it is done, so is that card. Toss it. You only have three left. Hold yourself to this principle, and you will begin to maximize the assignments you do grade at school to minimize the number of assignments you are grading overall. Do not take papers home to grade; grade papers at work where they belong. Also, simple hygiene note: the assignments you collect are a collection of bacteria, particles, and individualized germs from each and every student that handled it. Don't take that outside of the school building, into your car, your home, or your living room. And certainly, never grade papers in your bedroom. Leave work at work, and grading papers is definitely a big part of the work.

Master these three keys, and you will not be able to do any work at home because you don't have any, and you won't need a bag to carry it home in.

AFTER WORK

After work should be a time to release and return back to self. You should also allocate at least twenty solid minutes reflecting on your day: how it went, what went well, what could go better, your actions and

exchanges with staff and students, etc. Take some time each afternoon, maybe on the car ride home or after dinner before bed and before you complete your evening, to reflect over your day. Reflection in a profession is a significant trait to have. Reflection is a part of the profession. We should be thinking through all three realms, the present, the future, and the events of the past that have contributed. Each day has its own script. The hours in the day are the same each day, but they don't feel the same each day. Take the time to reflect on the hours and interactions that took place during that time each day can significantly enhance your practice. You must have time for the mind.

THE WEEKENDS

The weekends should be sacred. That time should be 100 percent for you and for your family. If you decide you want to do some work-related things, make sure it is because you would like to, not because you are stressed or pressed about them. Let pressing and stressing things remain in the schoolhouse and during the workweek. If it is because you are excited and eager to learn more about something, gain more practice with it, or it would bring you peace, then do it. Otherwise, the weekends are your time to recharge, rest, and refocus. They are not for extending the workweek into your home in efforts to get ahead of the next one. Release on the weekends. The weekends are for you, personally and professionally.

Professionally, it is important to have time turned off to recharge and refocus in order to be productive and at your best the following week. The weekends are mine. When it comes to the weekends, if there is something that you want to do, let it be things that are leisure and do not require much time – for example, reading a few chapters ahead in the novel your class is reading or reviewing the coming curriculum for the sake of reviewing and considering potential ideas, not unpacking or planning. These are simple and productive things to do over the weekend, comfortable on the couch or front porch. They are not completely consuming and should not take more than an hour. Always leverage the work time you are committing outside of work against family time and personal time you could be spending freely. I can sacrifice thirty minutes to an hour, maybe two if it is a really big project or idea I have, but after that, my time becomes costly. Try your best to let your weekends be free.

SELF-CARE PRACTICES
FOR THE PROFESSION

When it comes to caring for yourself professionally, you are caring for the parts of yourself and your body that allow you to be your best at your job. As a teacher, I like to focus on the area I use the most – my feet. I am standing on my feet a lot, and I am grateful that my feet are able to allow me to do things that I need to operate successfully. Because of this, I take good care of my feet. Caring for my feet and legs is a part of my self-care routine. Beyond getting pedicures, although I do love getting those, I take time after bathing to massage and moisturize my feet. I purchase shoes for work that will support and comfort my feet and legs as I work throughout the days. Investing in good shoes is an excellent tip as well. I have a set of comfortable shoes I keep under

my desk at all times to change into. Cute shoes are for cute things like walking the hallway and to and from your car. In the classroom practical shoes will see you through a longer way.

My mind is important, and being able to maintain my mental and emotional health is key for my ability to navigate and exchange interaction with my students and adult peers. That time my mind is "turned off" from work is important for my self-care routine. When I take mental health days – and I do take them mandatorily at least two times a year – I have learned to take two days and a weekend. Taking one day is not enough. If you can, take a Thursday and Friday off or a Friday and a Monday off. It takes one day to let your body and mind accept that it isn't actually at work or required to do anything. The second day you can actually rest or make any errands or appointments you want to do, but you need at least one whole day to let all the days prior to taking this intentional day of rest to release and roll off of you. Then you can rest and recharge. Then you can restart. When it comes to mental health days, take them in twos.

My spirit and joy levels are important for my ability to complete my job. If my joy is low and my spirit tattered with negativity, it presents obstacles that hinder me from being fluid and maximizing my energy efforts. Because of this, the time I spend doing things that I want to do freely and spending time with people and doing things that bring me joy and fill my spirit are important. It is important for the recharging factor. I have learned that Sundays are not for lesson planning and prepping for the week to come. That type of energy is depleting and should have already been spent the week prior because Monday should already be PPOPed and waiting for my arrival. Sundays are for deciding my week's wardrobe palette, preparing my lunch for the week, and preparing my bag for returning from the weekend. Sunday is for taking it slow and most importantly recharging and refilling my spirit. This day is reserved for doing things that rest and recharge the mind and spirit, not gear it up and cause anxiety for the coming week. Your energy is sacred, and it is key to the vessel that allows your passions to shine through. Be mindful.

Physically remember to mind your pace. How fast are your walking or rushing to and from your destinations? How quickly are you responding to things, emails, students? How quickly are you accepting new tasks and responsibilities before you know if you could handle them or not? My guess is pretty fast. Are you or do you feel like you are rushing everywhere? Slow down. Take your time walking just as you take your time in PPOPing and PIGing. One way I have found to impact the entire pace of how I am moving throughout the day was to slow down my walking. I tend to be a speedy walker, whether in a hurry or walking for pleasure. Slowing down my speed intentionally slowed down my pace, taking that moment to reform my hallway behavior, engage, and be present in conversations – not one foot present, one foot trailing off in my mind about the other tasks left to do – taking that time to be a listener, a person, a solution, or support.

A Few Professional Care Tips

- Lunch Kit: Keep a kit of supplies for eating and recess. A Ziploc of liquid condiments like ketchup and honey, another for dry like salt and pepper packets or containers, and a third full of utensils,

just in case. A few extra utensils and a few snacks. Energy requires fuel, right?

- Recess Kit: You should adapt to your climate. I live on the east coast in Maryland, and Maryland winters, falls, and early spring can be rainy, windy, and cold. Instead of toting gear for the weather back and forth or being cold during recess duty, I keep a set of recess weather gear at work at all times: a set of five-finger gloves, sunglasses, an extra scarf, and a sweater. I have a jumbo umbrella I keep in the closet in the event of a fire drill or some sort of emergency where we have to evacuate and be outside. Rarely are we required to stand in the rain. That job is reserved for the specialist and bus duty, thankfully. At my former schools, teachers did have to partake in bus duty rain or shine, and I was thankful for that jumbo and sturdy umbrella every time. I used to focus on the sleek, small, and cute ones until I got tired of fighting the wind for my umbrella. The wind won every time, succeeding in flipping my umbrella inverted, ferociously blowing it left-right and everywhere else but centered over me. Then when a student forgot his jumbo golf umbrella at the end of a school year, I grasped that thing and have held onto it ever since. I haven't had a need for it yet, but when I do… oh baby, will I be ready.

- Meal Tip: My final tip is do not skip breakfast. Do not skip over lunch. You will need the food to fuel the energy. Do not skip meals. It can be tempting, but do not skip breakfast; do not skip lunch. Sit down and stop. This is your time. Have breakfast each morning, and do not work through lunch.

OBSTACLES FOR THE NONBELIEVER

Now I am a real teacher, a true teacher, and I know how difficult it can be to walk away. When I first began pursuing the idea, I had a very hard and stumbling time initially. There is always something I am excited about or pressed about. There was always something I could talk or obligate myself into doing. I had to be strong. You will have to be strong. Trust me. In the beginning, fighting the urge to take something home was like fighting the urge to eat sugar. It feels impossible until it feels natural.

The ideas of 'no workbag' and 'no homework' are abstract at first. They sound dreamy, maybe unrealistic to you. That is fine for now. Dreams, if pursued, eventually come true. This can be done. It is done. I am by no means the first to discover this, and you will by no means be the last. We must discuss your biggest obstacle.

The biggest obstacle you will face is you. It is yourself. You are the person responsible for your outcomes; you are the one responsible for your input. Your biggest obstacle will be your ability to commit and remain consistent. It is important to note that your results will not be instant. This is a gradual process. In the beginning, the entire process of PPOPing will be time-consuming. You are retraining your mind, your routine, and your manner of practice. It is going to take you some time to learn, adjust, and then master, but mastery, efficiency, and simplicity will come. It took me years to realize what I needed and a couple more to learn how and then actually to do it. Take your time, and the investment will pay off.

The work bag – how do I leave my workbag at work? I will break this one down even further, but to keep it simple, ask yourself this

153

question before I answer: are you really going to need it? What do you need it for? If you have a physical planner, take your planner, but after that, do you need anything else? If most of your curriculum content is online and you are planning and grading at school, what else needs to come home that cannot be accessed online?

Commitment breeds results and flow. With continued practice, the time it takes to manage your workload will take less and less time, distinguishing between priority, immediately and mandatory. You must learn how to prioritize your priorities. Which are for that hour and the ones that can be done at later time periods or tackled together within the same day or time blocks? Can any be done at a later time within that same week? Take that time to evaluate, PIG before you accept additional responsibilities, and know that if you PPOPed in advance, most of the workload has been done for you.

Define your weekly routines and duties. Grading is something that is done weekly, so take care of that when you PPOP planning. Let's use one of my former school districts' grading policy as an example – teachers were required to input bi-weekly grades over an eight-week quarter four times a year. That is roughly sixteen grades a quarter. Knowing that number is significant because when you are planning, you pulled out the grades you would be collecting. Now you know exactly how many grades you will need at a minimum. Plan productively, and when you are pulling your grades, be strategic and account for them as a part of your district minimum. If you are completing three units a quarter, that is about five to six grades each unit you intend to receive and grade. Make your grades count. How many group-work projects and assessments? How many homework grades if you implement home-work? How many are classwork grades? What do those grades belong to –vocabulary, assignment sheets evaluations, assessments? Consider these things while you are planning to organize your grading so that it is productive and intentional. You do not have to grade everything. Prioritize the most meaningful grades first, then consider adding addi-tional assignments to grade after.

Another routine duty is printing copies and making resources. Again, you did the bulk of this already when you compiled your print list and created your resources during your planning. This should be as simple as sliding the documents through and pressing print. When you are organizing and preparing to productive, you should have or will be tackling the work you have to do as far as preparing for your coming week. That too has been done for you. That initial PPOP is the hardest one, but once you begin and set the foundations for the routine process, it will become much smoother. You will establish your own sophisticated flow.

The rest of this process is a mentality. You have to want to be able to be successful at work and get back to yourself and then believe that you will achieve that. Period. Establish clear and defined lines for yourself and boundaries for others. Things will feel different at first, and there may be people who do not understand your new focus or manner of practice. You cannot let that deter you. Commitment and consistency. You have to set the goal for yourself. I have provided you the plan.

CHAPTER 8

CHAPTER 8

"Give Me Recess or Give Me Retirement"
– Exiting and Transitions

Journal Entry: March 16, 2017

"This is a God Dream being Fulfilled

I want to leave respected and valued for myself. For the quality, character, talented ability that I am. For the woman and person, the human being that I am. Miss Felton. That name has great meaning, great value, great time.

This is a God Dream.

I do not intend to stay here long. I will not be here much longer. In fact, my time could be due. But in the few final moments I have, it does not mean I cannot be my absolute best.

Legacy. I came here from a dream. I am living the Dream.

Amen."

At some point in your career, you are going to come to a point where you are considering making a career move. It may be a move out of the classroom into another position or something as simple as a grade change. No matter what or how the change is being made, there will come a point in your career you and the others around you will transition and/or leave. Things do not stay the same forever. That's alright. That is a good thing; change is inevitable, and with change always comes opportunity. If it is a teammate, a colleague, or you, always celebrate and look for the positive in what is to come.

Keep a similar mentality for all other coworkers and colleagues, even the ones you do not favor as much. Let any emotions arise, release them, and then politely congratulate them in goodwill. There is no need to hold grudges in the workplace, especially not in this profession. We each depend on each other for something at some point, oftentimes more than once. Keep a duly noted mental note, but don't hold it against or brand it to their name how they did you unjustly or offensively.

Remember our principles: *we forgive and let go because we are one big educational schoolhouse family*. You may, and more than likely will, come across this person again – whether it be at a conference, an email, a cohort you join later in your career. You just never know, but what you can know is that it sucks to get a jolt of anger every time you see this person unexpectedly across the room or see their name in a group email. If you chose to professionally address it, address it; otherwise, release it. Let it go. Pent-up resentment causes indigestion and anxiety. Wish them well and smile. You may no longer have to deal with or see them daily, and that may be a really good thing. No matter what, wish them well with an open and clean heart.

LOSING COWORKERS AND PROMOTION OF OTHERS

I believe the hardest coworker to lose or see rise above you sometimes is not your enemy but your best work friend. Do you have one? Are you guilty of being one? The day will come when your work best friend has decided that they would like to work at a new school or switch to a new position where you will no longer have the comforts of each other to lean on. It will suck and may feel like you two are "breaking up" at first, and you may want to fall victim to your emotions – jealousy, maybe loss, maybe even anger.

Have them, let them rise up, let tears roll out, and release them. It is okay to feel the emotions, and it is okay to have them. Do not feel guilty about having them either; you are human, after all. You are also not alone. No matter how well we get along with someone or wish them well when they decide they are going to move forward and go places that we are not going it does feel… even if it is just for a brief moment… like they are leaving us. And that's fair. You have probably been used to seeing each other and interacting with each other every Monday through Friday consistently for the last several years.

Sometimes, our fears of losing our coworkers come from the fear of not being able to relate and have things to talk about outside of the job. Sure, you catch each other up on a few shallow life events on Mondays after the weekends and discuss the latest trending media, but realistically, this is a surface-level friendship, working well together and enjoying the time spent together productively or nonproductively with the mass of your relationship and conversations having to do with what you do at the job are circumstantial. But coworker friends can actually be real friends, and you don't have to 'break up' because your locations have changed. You just have to be intentional about discussing and relating to each other on other topics beyond the job.

Real relationships can be formed. That is why it is okay to allow yourself to feel selfish emotions first. Then release those feelings, accept that your coworker friend is going to be leaving you soon, and get over there to congratulate your work best friend honestly and whole-heartedly. What is real is real, and you will easily see if you had a real relationship if once the job is done you no longer have anything in common or to talk about.

I have had the honor of forming many great relationships and one really good friend that started out as a coworker. We met as members of the same team and obviously related to the daily routines and students we shared as teammates. Most of my career was spent working alongside her, and as far as I knew it, that was what I expected. And then one year when the day came and we were broken-up, separated by grade levels, it actually was alright – upsetting but alright. We had taken the time to establish a relationship outside of school and also discussed topics that had nothing to do with school and instead were about our personal lives. We built a real friendship that could stand whether we worked together or not. Interestingly enough – both of us busy bees – since our grade changes, we hardly speak in school beyond hallway hellos and quick room pop-ins. When we get together now, we have so much more to talk about. Never worry; be able to identify the situation and reasons for your emotions and address them accordingly.

PROMOTION OF OTHERS

"They got the job I wanted." Those words right there. I have seen those six words end relationships and ruin a person's entire spirit. Here

come six more, "They liked them better than me." This section honestly hurts a little to write, but it is my duty to keep it plain for you.

Dear teacher, my dearest one, do you know you are a superstar?
Because that is the first part of this section. You have to know that fact
humbly first. You are a superstar teacher. Whatever it may be that you
do not know and wherever you do not shine presently, you have the
skills and talent to find out and grow. You are a star teacher because
your passions and devotions to the job radiate from within. That is
something you own and developed on your own – there is no position
or job title necessary to validate that.

With that being said, let's go back to the initial six words. When you
first read those statements, I am sure you *read* into them too, adding
emotion and context. Now let's add some math in. We are going to
go back to the original statements and do some subtracting. Instead
of "They got the job I wanted," which may imply that something was
taken from you, consider taking your emotions out of the statement
and accepting the promotion as a fact, "They got the job." Instead of
"They liked them better than me," which can be a completely unfair
and selfish statement to assume, consider "Are my pursuits aligned
here?" Mathematically speaking, these statements are now more concrete. Just as you subtracted those few words from each original statement, subtract the feelings too.

While I will always contest that teachers, of all kinds, are the most
important beings on the planet; in the schoolhouse, it is the students.
The students are always number one! And that's the point and a part
of the reason you choose to be there each day. It would be naive to

say that politics do not sometimes play a part. However, staffing decisions are made based on the individual needs of the student body. It isn't personal; it is professional. Don't allow professional decisions that disappoint you to discourage you. They should motivate you to make beneficial and logical professional decisions as well. This just could be the subtle boost you needed in disguise.

"What if I want to know why?" are the seven curious words of our hearts. This question, no matter how bothered or unbothered you are about staffing or even student transitions, is one that all of us ask about something at least a few times. Personally, I think that is okay and completely natural. I think it is completely normal to have a curiosity about why or how someone may have been promoted. It can be great information. I think the motives behind the inquiry are of the most significance. It's okay to want to know why, but why do you want to know why? Is it constructive, and how are will it be useful? "Am I interested in gaining the information for my personal gains? Does this new information benefit my professional promotion or thoughts of change? Or am I just curious, and once I acquire said information, I'll have very little use for it so I'll end up passing it along as gossip – something we discussed as being seriously unproductive and a time-waster?

On the other hand, there are the times when that seven-word question must undyingly be answered. You just have to know. There is a certain manner in which I recommend you go about it. Before I begin, I have to provide another disclaimer. I've experienced the seven worded inquiry, but I didn't handle it the way I am going to offer you do at first. For me, it was the situation I learned from.

Time for a story!

I have asked the seven worded question about staffing once, so far, in my career. I mentioned that I had the opportunity to spend most of my career working alongside a good teammate. I briefly stated that when I was transitioned to a new team and grade the experience was initially upsetting. Well, that was skipping a few details. The principal we had at the time was fair and shared this new information with me privately. When I was first informed that the transition would be made and I was going to be the one who would be making it, I stuck to script and did what I would normally do, accept the information and decision professionally but do not respond emotionally. So, I smiled, I nodded, and I said thank you. It was obvious the meeting had come to a close, so I began to walk out the door to begin to accept the information I'd received. Somewhere along the way, between my feet and my exit, I realized I couldn't accept this one professionally.

Before my foot could hit the doorway, I turned around and asked why. If my memory serves me, my exact words were, "But why? Please tell me *your* why." I couldn't help it. I wasn't going to be able to just process this one out. When I turned, it wasn't *Miss Felton*; it was *Danielle* asking why. It wasn't that I was being transitioned. That would have been fine if my *friend* was coming too. Sure, it would have been senseless and irritating to us, maybe everybody, but that was the point. This was an emotional thing a personal response.

I wasn't asking as the professional who knew that ultimately, I would adjust and be fine. I was the person who felt like they were being snatched away from their friend. That was the emotion that compelled me to

stop and ask, but there was also some professional logic too. This transition was going to disrupt and change my entire system of normal. This also meant that I would now have to learn three new curriculums and a new student dynamic in addition to adjusting to a new team. The entire impact of that news was a bummer and stung when it first hit.

Unintentionally, I realized the bee in me sent that sting right back when I asked, and my principal's eyes immediately opened wide. I walked away from the second round of our conversation understanding two things. The first was that there is a reason why I try to always keep it sophisticated and professional. The second, my principal was not prepared for their answer. Again, I thanked them, I smiled, I nodded. This time, I made it through the door.

It didn't matter what their answer was, and if you asked me, I wouldn't even be able to remember. That was what I learned. It wasn't that they did not know the answer or how to answer. It was that my principal was not *prepared* to respond with an answer at that time. See how important it is to PPOP!

That was the second thing I learned – the reasoning behind why it is important to keep it sophisticated and professional in the schoolhouse always, sophisticated at least. After our meeting and after reflecting and processing, or PIGing, through my personal feelings and re-centering on my practice, I realized all would be well. My teammate happens to also be a friend in real life, and I would be fine. My comfort zone was getting ready to be disrupted, and that is not always a bad thing. Finally, don't roll your eyes on this next one, embrace it as a part of your practice too.

"I am Miss Felton. That means that I am a superstar teacher. Anything that I do not know how to do I have the ability and skills to develop and find. I discover and create the tools I will need to thrive. I've got this. I can handle it. I grow, glow and let go." This is why it is so important to shine from the inside out (refer back to Chapter 7 if you need). You are in charge of and responsible for the magnificence you have within. I just needed to remind myself of that.

From the perspective of the school and the principal, it all made sense, and that is what mattered in this situation. I understood that once I took the personal out and realized it did make sense and was well-thought-out in terms of students. To be fair, a week or so later I saw my principal coming down the hallway. My normal custom being is to greet and smile, so the fact that it appeared that they were walking towards me didn't even occur to me until they were standing directly infront of me. My principal stopped and asked if we could follow up on our last conversation.

I'd already come to terms with the change. This conversation went much more smoothly and simply because I had already processed through my PIG, and they had time to PPOP for it. I also apologized not for my emotions or questioning but for my process. After reflection, I realized that part, my process for asking, was unfair. Before the meeting closed, we both smiled, we nodded, and we thanked each other. I made it smoothly through the exit threshold without stopping and anticipated the following year to go well. I had the secrets to PPOP and PIG through the rest.

CLOSING CHAPTERS
KNOWING WHEN TO LEAVE AND
EXIT PLANNING

Before we close this chapter, you know I couldn't send you off without a good plan. This section is broken into three parts and two plans. The first plan is the ideal exit plan for when you are able to choose it's time to leave the classroom. The second plan is the plan for when circumstance requires you to leave the classroom.

KNOWING WHEN TO LEAVE

You know when you are ready to leave when you know. That is my most accurate answer. Everyone's reasoning will be different – career reasons, personal reasons, or emergency reasons. Even if you fight it, when the time comes, you will know it, and it will be a reason that is very personal and unique to you and your ability. You will know when it is time to physically leave.

How do you know when that time is near? When that dismissal bell begins to ring deep down in the pit of your belly. It is a process, a soft-sounding and slowly ringing bell that gets ignored or acknowledged and then over time begins to start increasing in volume, then in speed and rigor. It's the internal dismissal bell. I've been in more modern schools that have school bells that are actually beeps released over the intercom. Those students miss out on that old school elation, thrill, and slight fright middle school kids got when that bronze golden bell would ring. Sorry for the people sitting underneath it or close by. Their poor ears. Take the good feelings about the bell and flip them to negative anxious ones that don't stop and increase a little bit each day. When your internal bell begins ringing, it is time to address the bell or prepare for departure.

Should you choose to move on, move out, or change careers, there should be one thing you absolutely make your priority if nothing else – to leave clean. Leave with a clean space, a clean conscience, and an as-clean-as-you-can reputation. Leave in good will knowing that you have done your best, committed your best, and now it is time to do what is best for you. Be confident and guilt-free once you have made your decision and commit to it.

It can be tempting to turn back and hard to not waver especially when you have the connections and built the relationships with students, staff, and families over the years. You will be making a choice, the choice to remain or to change make a change, to be comfortable or to be uncomfortable. Make and commit to the one that your heart says yes to. Your gut, your fears, and your mind may reason out reasons. You've got this. If you spent your time well and you do leave clean, should ever you decide to return, you will always be in good standing with your school. Remember, what is real is real. Real relationships are lasting.

EXIT PLANNING PLAN A AND PLAN B

I do not hope to advocate for or promote quitting teaching and leaving your job. This is a book about how to stay and remain a teacher, after all, but I will always advocate and promote you making the best decisions for you and your career. Please don't leave, but if you do leave, clean and leave with a plan.

◊ PLAN A: TRANSITIONS AT THE END OF THE SCHOOL YEAR

The moment you have confirmed within yourself before you have said anything outwardly that you will be leaving, you begin cleaning. I mention "leave clean," and I am referring to a clean spirit primarily, but within this context, I mean clean.

Start throwing out, donating, giving, and clearing out unnecessary paper and waste items. Resourceful materials that other staff or the school can use that you are not keeping provide, deliver or leave to the staff. If there are things that are yours or you have permission to give away, give them to the students if that will benefit them academically – not things like toys but things like snacks, books, magazines, or kits, if you have permission and can distribute equitably, not on a favoritism basis. Your goal should be to always leave a place better than it was when you came, metaphorically and physically.

Next, set the incoming or remaining persons up for success. Again, what you don't need and would be productive or useful for the next year, consider leaving, but do not leave behind junk or things just because you could not part with it yourself. A simple rule of thumb is if you didn't use it, why would they? If it is over five years old, it's probably out of date curriculum-standard-wise, so it would be the best use as practice. You can consider that a waste too.

Third, if you are responsible for any teams, clubs, or committees, before the end of the year, start preparing the next person or process for the next person to take over. Begin compiling and organizing the necessary information they will need. Make the transferring of goodwill and information from how you did things become less specific to you and more transferable and adaptive to incoming parties. Start minimizing your leadership roles and responsibilities to ones that are more specific to the transition you are trying to make so that the staff is less likely to feel deficient from your lack of presence.

Finally, as you begin the process and processing your time before departure, remember to be respectful of others and their feelings, not so much opinions. You do not always know how much your presence may mean to somebody or how much it meant to somebody else for them to be getting that position instead of you. No guilty feelings; gratitude only. No matter what, you will certainly be missed. When the year ends, use the PPOP process to pack up.

◊ PLAN B: TRANSITIONS DURING THE SCHOOL YEAR

This transition usually is the harder one to make, primarily because of the cost of impact. The effects of a teacher leaving during a school year can sometimes be irreparable. That is not to guilt or shame anyone considering or who has had to make this decision. It is just a fact. Leaving in the middle of an ongoing school year is going to have a cost of impact, and that impact directly affects the students first, usually then trickling down on to staff. It's the circle of the schoolhouse. Anything that impacts the students leads you right back to a teacher. When you leave, a part of your impact is the effect you cause on the other teachers on your team. Again, no guilt, no shame. This is another cost of impact effect fact. The steps for plan B are primarily centered around those two impact costs. The currency, your time and energy. The process is similar to plan A with small differences.

First, the moment you find out or have the inkling that your circumstances may be causing you to leave the classroom, incrementally or permanently, you begin the minimalizing clean and clear out process. Don't move frantically or drastically because that may disrupt the class culture and upset students. Follow the guidelines of your district, but I would wait to inform students until things are concrete and a plan has been put into place. Try to keep things as close to looking and functionally like normal as possible. This means that your room on the surface will basically function and look the same. Some may say it seems "lighter in here; something is different." That just means the junk is gone.

Next, start setting the next person, your classroom, and your students up for success. This is the meat of the plan. You have to leave, you will be missed, and you will miss it all too. How you leave is how you avoid the guilt. Set them up for success as best you can.

1. Begin delegating classroom responsibilities to students where you can. For example, if you watered the plant and stacked the chairs at the end of the day, assign the plant as a job and have each student responsible for flipping their own chair during dismissal before they leave. These examples are petty, but the point is to think of simple jobs you take on for your classroom that the students could potentially take over without instructional impact so that the next teacher has a few fewer things to worry about and a system already established for them.

2. Start transitioning the class culture. If your class culture was one that was very reliant on your leadership, begin transitioning leadership

and responsibility accountably to the students. Encourage student thinking to shift from "we follow rules because our teacher made them" to "we follow rules because they benefit us and our academic culture." This may sound complicated, but it is a matter of taking time to start identifying the leadership qualities in your students and promoting a "community" and "we do" attitude. This yields the best results when you have already fostered these qualities into your class culture so that you can with this pending change now focus on promoting and not building them.

3. Begin minimizing things related to your class culture that are specific to you. That means if in my classroom, I ran a classroom ticket economy, I would be phasing that process out before the incoming teacher. Students will still hold on to things they love and the next person may like the idea, but if it is something that is a part of your class culture that is not mandatory and requires the next person to learn it, consider phasing it out. You can leave instructions behind if you feel compelled.

4. Finally, be respectful and as mindful as you can about the feelings of the other people and children around you. Your impact and your gift are to things that could never be replaced.

Leaving in the middle of the school year not always but usually is something that cannot wait. With that being said, if you can, try to at least always say thank you, goodbye and leave a smile's worth of good memories.

CHAPTER 9

"Over the Hill or over the Mountain We Conquer Both Together!"

– Obstacles You May Face and How to Overcome Them

Oh, the endeavor of the teacher. It is a great duty you have taken on, one that is respected and honored. Not everyone can be a teacher. Not everyone can teach. To teach is to do, to create, and to be. So when teaching, as in most things in life, you are going to come across obstacles and challenges. One of your greatest obstacles is going to be you – more specifically, your ability to commit to the idea that, yes, it is possible to accomplish my work tasks within my workday each week and the belief that it is you who can make that happen.

However, there may be days when even the most optimistic mind just can't shake that funky, overwhelmed feeling. You are not alone in this temporary mood, and you don't have to venture into PPOPing alone. When I first began this process, I began it alone. As time went on, I realized this job is best done in community! You have the tools not only for you but for a whole team to divide amongst themselves.

You can PPOP out a whole school year before the kids even start. It would definitely take a lot of preparation and organization, but the planning is something you already know how to do and would each be doing on your own anyway. Why not simplify the process and do it together and more productively?

It's an idea, but if you don't have the support of a team or you are your own one-member production, you should know that you will always be welcomed into our sophisticated community of teachers. But, although our arms are welcoming, there is a high cost to stay. You must be passionate about the part you play in this profession, loyal to your process of change, willing to work hard, of course, and committed to sharing the laughs along the way. Your commitment to sharing and indulging in joy is going to be one of the highest costs you will have to pay. This is because sharing your joy and indulging in the joy of others takes time and requires effort, compassion, and sacrifice. You may have to humble yourself, do things you don't want to do, or be drawn into conversations you don't want to hear. So what?

Refer back to our principle rules. Remember "we care for each other as if we are each other as if it were us caring for us ourselves." That doesn't mean carrying people on your back – it means lifting them up when they're down and feeling mediocre. To stay in joy, you have to find and surround yourself with joy. It's an internal key, one that's stamped *arrived* and releases joy when you unlock the door of *feelings of home* we carry with us wherever we go. We love to be surrounded by people and things we love at home. So, in the same way, we must invest and put efforts forth into our real homes; we must incorporate and foster that same energy in our internal and professional homes. Start fostering those professional home vibes now, and don't forget that laughter is a cheat code that always works!

Whether we know it or not, it's that silent key to the joy that unlocks our passions for what we do each day. Some may unlock it the moment they wake or when the hot drink kicks in. Others may unlock it the moment their students arrive. Once upon a time, you may have referred to this as your "on" mode, or worse, your "mask," the *"I've got this all under control. I'm in charge. I'm ready to serve and excited to be here"* facade. It's not that it's untrue – it's that it is fake. That "on" you were symbolizing was the mask of confidence, security, and joy. It's okay if you've had to fake it every once in a while – we've all had to fake or force ourselves through the funk too. But too much faking starts to poison you and become unhealthy.

To be in joy doesn't mean to have things perfect or to be positive all the time. It's the home state of feeling comfort, peace, and pleasure. Joy comes from the inside-out, not the outside-in. With all that being said, I reiterate – your biggest obstacle will be you and your ability to share and indulge in joy like that of a child living out their dreams every Monday through Friday, summers and weekends included.

This book is a resource for conquering your work obstacles and barriers so that you can get back to your passions and joys. I've shared with you my secrets, tips, and a few stories between these pages together with you, so you can own your own journey and joy. Believe and know that nothing and no one can take that from you. It is now up to you to implement what you've learned and become it.

You now have the guides and the frameworks to reassess and simplify your work life, as well as how to PPOP and PIG in all things and get your workload under control and out of your way so you can live a fulfilling life full of what you make it. You hold your own keys.

BEFORE YOU GO

I hope with my guides and these frameworks you will be able and well-equipped as you set off each day. Be my guest in establishing a community of celebration and joy with teachers who are also PPOPing and sharing their renewed joys within their careers. Share the secret and your joy as you collaborate to build healthy, passionate, and joy-filled educator communities at your schools, with teachers in your professional and personal life too!

You are also welcome to join our growing community of PPOPing teachers and educators. Be warned, it is a part of our communal culture where we encourage, uplift, and hold each other accountable for knocking out our workloads *within* the workweek and getting back to our lives and enjoying our career and passions again. You can find out more or stay up to date about how to *Teach and Go Home* and our passionate community of educators who have mastered simplifying and sophisticated their work lives by emailing at TeachGoHome@gmail.com.

There you can also find out how to gain access to planning matrixes, classroom organization models, and other resources accessible for you. I can't wait for you to begin implementing and share how you have redesigned your workload and are balancing all of your new free time and passions.

TIPS TO PROSPER

- This process will take time and effort, but it will be totally worth it!

- Consider the work and time you put in upfront as an investment. You want to get a huge bang for your buck!

- Stay committed to yourself and your process of change in order to cash out big!

- You will have days when you fall off the plan. The increase in your workload will alert you of this for sure. That is okay, you can PIG to get in-sync and PPOP again.

- Joy is best served when it has been warmed from within. Protect your source and nurture your glow always.

- Do not skip your meals – make them something to look forward to, and get plenty of rest each night. It's the fuel for your mind. Recharge to your spirit – you will need it to conquer each day.

- Establish a work playlist to blast and charge you up on your way to work. Be mindful of what you choose.

If you would like more information about personal coaching or consulting on how to implement your sophisticated and simplified process, you can contact me directly via email at defppop@gmail.com for consultations and conversations.

CHAPTER 10

CHAPTER 10

"Dismissal Bell Rings"
– The Conclusion

Now we have reached the end. I was able to write this manuscript for you because I enjoy and absolutely love what I do. It would have been quite the task to prioritize the time otherwise. I wrote this book with the aspirations of using my experiences to solve this question for you: *"How do I accomplish my workload and actually get things done at work so I can get back to enjoying teaching and my life?"*

The resolve to this problem would be worth its value of time. Gaining and maximizing much of the valuable time, teachers need to put more passion and effficiency into planning, getting back to enjoying their students growths in learning, and reflecting on their practice and the time to complete the task assigned for that day within that date. I hope to have given you a guide to managing what can sometimes feel like an overwhelming amount of responsibility and redundancy. I hope to not just provide you with a resource but also a conversation with a real teacher. No, not someone with false optimism or a reference guide that takes you right back to where you started – a real teacher who has been to places of failure and built the pathways back to success.

My wish is that you can use the information in this book as a framework to simplify and achieve your professional goals with ease, efficiency, and organization. Now, you should be able to tap back into your passion and inspiration behind teaching to convey your talent and beauty for the profession with ease.

I hope you have enjoyed this conversation and experience. I want you to feel rejuvenated and re-inspired to re-conquer your profession, equipped with the tools and wisdom needed to build your confidence. We need to re-inspire teacher value and our appreciation for each other and the uniquely designed job we do each and every Monday through Friday.

Each of our experiences will be unique, but our goals are the same – to identify our shared obstacles in teaching and develop systems to efficiently, effectively, and realistically overcome each one. You have been introduced to the outline and framework for how and what it means to PPOP and prepare your planning sessions in an organized and productive manner. You have also learned the prerequisites (or post) to teaching that no one told you about.

We take our time discussing the simplified methods for constructing our classroom layouts so that they are purposeful, efficient, and easy. Now you have an idea of how to navigate the student, staff, parent, and email juggle in ways that are thoughtful and keep you clear-minded.

If nothing else, I hope you gained a few neat ideas and have heard my cry for balance, simplicity, and function. You understand now the benefits of balancing your professional and personal life and how to do it without stressing yourself out. What is done is done, and that is okay.

Now, if you reach and decide to make a change, you will always make them clean and smiling. When others do the same, we smile for them too. I can't wait to see you in the field, and I look forward to changing the world with you. Teach on, shine, and prosper, great mind — the future is counting on us!

Acknowledgments

I would like to thank each and every educator who took the time to step into the classroom to teach me. I may not have appreciated it then, and I am sure I didn't say it, but thank you for picking up the pen and pencil to serve.

I have to give a special thank you to my Gator, Wildcat, and Nighthawk families. Without the experiences, challenges, and love, I would not have been able to do all that I set out to do. My sincerest gratitude to my VES family and the fifth-grade team. I love you all more than I will ever have the words to express. Thank you for nurturing me, pushing me, and being a part of my journey.

To my awesome and amazing family – I thank you and thank you again for your love, encouragement, and phenomenal support. Thank you also to my extended family and friends for their support. I look forward to the next chapters.

Above all else, I would like to give my thanks and praise to God. Father, I thank you for leading and nurturing me always. Thank you to The Author Incubator and their course in the Author's Way for the journey we embarked on together and your guiding hands along the way. I am so grateful that He led us together.

Thank You for Reading

Thank you for taking the time to read *Teach and Go Home: The Sophisticated Guide to Simplifying and Managing Your Workload and More.* I hope you enjoyed the conversation and gained a few things to share with other teachers and educators too. With sincerest gratitude, I would love to offer you a free gift and the opportunity to continue the conversation. By sending an email to TeachGoHome@gmail.com with the Subject line "Hello Teacher! More Please" I will know to send you our free PPOP gift.

If you already know you are certain and ready to cut the distractions, frustrations, and time wasting, and return to joy right now, there is something for you too! The opportunity to take the *Teach and Go Home* process to the next level and have a one to one experience implementing the strategies and practices. You can find out more about the sophisticating your process exclusively, by emailing defppop@gmail.com.

Thank you for teaching!

About the Author

MISS DANIELLE E. FELTON, author of *Teach and Go Home*, is a passionate and faith-driven educator. Born and raised on the eastern coast, she is currently living in Maryland. Stemming from a line of educators, Danielle has been immersed in the field of education in education since childhood. It was the summers during her teenage years spent volunteering at the early education childhood center for children with disabilities and special needs her mother worked at that cemented her love for teaching and children, describ-

ing the experience as where she was able to witness the true 'magic' of educators and fall in love with the significance of education, watching teaching that went beyond academics and focusing specifically on the learning, growth, and the students. However, it was a passion for the elementary classroom that called to 'Miss Felton's' heart. Danielle has worked professionally in the field of education for almost ten years and has worked as an elementary school teacher for the last six. Although teaching has been a dream since childhood, Danielle's true passions belong to service, development, and people. Danielle is on course to completing a master's degree in educational leadership spring of 2021 with future plans in the field of education that will impact not only the way teachers teach but the entire system of how we are doing it.

About Difference Press

Difference Press is the exclusive publishing arm of The Author Incubator, an educational company for entrepreneurs – including life coaches, healers, consultants, and community leaders – looking for a comprehensive solution to get their books written, published, and promoted. Its founder, Dr. Angela Lauria, has been bringing to life the literary ventures of hundreds of authors–in–transformation since 1994.

A boutique–style self–publishing service for clients of The Author Incubator, Difference Press boasts a fair and easy–to–understand profit structure, low–priced author copies, and author–friendly contract terms. Most importantly, all of our #incubatedauthors maintain ownership of their copyright at all times.

LET'S START A MOVEMENT WITH YOUR MESSAGE

In a market where hundreds of thousands of books are published every year and are never heard from again, The Author Incubator is different. Not only do all Difference Press books reach Amazon bestseller status, but all of our authors are actively changing lives and making a difference.

Since launching in 2013, we've served over 500 authors who came to us with an idea for a book and were able to write it and get it self-published in less than 6 months. In addition, more than 100 of those books were picked up by traditional publishers and are now available in book stores. We do this by selecting the highest quality and highest potential applicants for our future programs.

Our program doesn't only teach you how to write a book – our team of coaches, developmental editors, copy editors, art directors, and marketing experts incubate you from having a book idea to being a published, bestselling author, ensuring that the book you create can actually make a difference in the world. Then we give you the training you need to use your book to make the difference in the world, or to create a business out of serving your readers.

ARE YOU READY TO MAKE A DIFFERENCE?

You've seen other people make a difference with a book. Now it's your turn. If you are ready to stop watching and start taking massive action, go to http://theauthorincubator.com/apply/.

"Yes, I'm ready!"

Other Books by Difference Press

The Top 1% Life: The Real Estate Agent's Guide to Free Up Your Time, Build Your Business with Confidence, and Finally, Have a Life Outside of Sales! by Kathleen Black

Get Back to Living: Navigating Through the Loss of Your Spouse by Allison L. Brown

Stop Worrying about Your Anxious Child: How to Manage Your Child's Anxiety so You Can Finally Relax by Tonya C. Crombie, Ph.D.

Become a Badass Rebel Runner: The Ultimate Guide to Being a Fit Mom without the Diet Bullshit by Jane Elizabeth

From Borderline to Baseline: 9 Key Steps to Manage Your BPD and Start Loving Your Life by Julie Ann Ford

Stop Draining Your Energy: The Movement Teacher's Guide to Attract Clients You Love by Heather Glidden

Is This Sickness or an Energy Block?: Know the Difference and What to Do about It by Amy Keast

Should I Leave My Relationship or Not?: The Smart Woman's Guide to a Clear Path Forward by Karen Lin

Side Hustle to Main Hustle: The Corporate Woman's Guide to Full-Time Entrepreneurship by Angel N. Livas

The Spiritual Entrepreneur: Quantum Leap Into Your Next Level of Impact and Abundance by Angelina Lombardo

Invention Protection Strategies: Expose Your Intellectual Property and Fund Your Startup by Cynthia Lombardo

Reverse Heart Disease Naturally: The Woman's Guide to Not Die before Your Time by Laurie Morse

Know What You Want Next: Break Free of the 'I Don't Know' Trap and Love Your Life Again by Kimberly Napier

Build Your Business with Social Media: The Step-by-Step Guide to Create a Life You Love by Gry Sinding

Should I Leave Nursing?: 7 Steps to Career Clarity by Karen Beck Wade, Ph.D.

Made in the USA
Coppell, TX
09 May 2022